THE
DEPOPULATION
IMPERATIVE

HOW MANY
PEOPLE CAN
EARTH SUPPORT?

T0359980

Paul Collins is an historian, broadcaster and writer. A Catholic priest for thirty-three years, he resigned from the active ministry in 2001 following a dispute with the Vatican over his book *Papal Power* (1997). He is the author of fifteen books. A former head of the religion and ethics department of the Australian Broadcasting Corporation, he is well known as a commentator on Catholicism and the papacy, as well as religious, environmental and population issues. www.paulcollinscatholicwriter.com.au

Also by Paul Collins

Mixed Blessings
No Set Agenda
God's Earth
Papal Power
Upon This Rock
The Modern Inquisition
Hell's Gates
Burn
Between the Rock and a Hard Place
Believers
God's New Man
Judgment Day
The Birth of the West
Absolute Power
A Very Contrary Irishman

THE
DEPOPULATION
IMPERATIVE

HOW MANY
PEOPLE CAN
EARTH SUPPORT?

PAUL COLLINS

Australian Scholarly

© 2021 Paul Collins

Published 2021 by
Australian Scholarly Publishing Ltd
7 Lt Lothian St Nth, North Melbourne, Vic 3051
Tel: 03 9329 6963 / Fax: 03 9329 5452
enquiry@scholarly.info / www.scholarly.info

ISBN 978-1-922669-21-6

Cover Design: Wayne Saunders, Matilda Heeps

Contents

Acknowledgements

I first wrote about overpopulation in 1994 in my book *God's Earth*, and it has remained a preoccupation for me ever since. But it was joining the organization Sustainable Population Australia (SPA) back in the mid-1990s that really helped me understand our massive impact on the planet.

At first, I was interested in Australia's carrying capacity, that is how many people can the island continent sustain while retaining its ecological integrity, and my sympathy was with those – like Tim Flannery – who argue that the country is already overpopulated. Also, talking to fellow SPA patrons, the distinguished virologist, Professor Frank Fenner (died 2010) and Dr Mary White (died 2018), Australia's premier paleobotanist, convinced me that world overpopulation was the most pressing issue facing us as humankind. It was Jenny Goldie, national president of SPA, who asked me to join the distinguished group who were patrons of SPA, an honour that I still value deeply. Jenny has worked for many years to keep the overpopulation message in the media and public consciousness. The Hon. Sandra Kanck, former president of SPA, and former Democrats' leader, Senator John Coulter, have also worked extremely hard to keep this issue in public consciousness. I am indebted to them all for their friendship and advice. (To understand why I value SPA so highly, see my comments at www.population.org.au/video/meet-spa-patrons.) Two other distinguished Australians who have influenced my views on the environment are my friends, former Green Senators Christine Milne and Bob Brown.

The person who suggested the idea of this book was my friend, Tom Hayes who reminded me of the priority of the natural world and biodiversity by putting earth first. Tom suggested that we needed a whole new approach that prioritized nature and it was his comments that spurred me to write this book. Thanks also to Nick Walker and the wonderful staff at Australian Scholarly; it has been a real pleasure to work with you through successive COVID-19 Melbourne lockdowns.

Inevitably there will be errors of fact and interpretation because I have stayed out of my primary area of expertise – history and religion – into various scientific disciplines. Any mistakes are my responsibility entirely.

Paul Collins
Canberra, ACT
August 2021

Abbreviations

AD	*Anno domini*—the period after the birth of Christ
AIDS	acquired immunodeficiency syndrome
BC	the period before the birth of Christ
BSE	bovine spongiform encephalopathy (mad cow disease)
C	Celsius
CDR	carbon dioxide removal
CE	Common era—the period after the birth of Christ
CELAM	Latin American and Caribbean Bishops Conferences
DESA	UN's Department of Economic and Social Affairs
FAO	Food and Agriculture Organization (UN)
GFC	global financial crisis
GFN	Global Footprint Network
GM	genetic modification (of plants)
HIV	human immunodeficiency virus
IPBES	Intergovernmental Science-Policy Platform on Biodiversity and Ecosystem Services Report (6 May 2019)
IPCC	Intergovernmental Panel on Climate Change
IPPF	International Planned Parenthood Federation
IUCN	International Union for the Conservation of Nature
IUD	inter uterine device
LIA	Little Ice Age
LS	the encyclical *Laudato si'* (25 May 2015)
MRSA	Methicillin-resistant staphylococcus aureus (staph bacteria resistant to antibiotics)
OECD	Organization for Economic Co-operation and Development
SARS	severe acute respiratory syndrome
SRM	solar radiation management
UNESCO	UN Education, Scientific and Cultural Organization
Vatican I	Second Vatican Council (1962–65)
WCC	World Council of Churches
WHO	World Health Organization
WWF	World Wildlife Fund
YBP	years before the present
ZPG	zero population growth

Introduction—Coronavirus

It may seem an odd place to start a book about population, but the COVID-19 pandemic actually leads us right into the heart of the issue. Virological experts have been warning for years that a highly infectious disease of some sort would almost certainly hit us and with COVID-19 their predictions have been realized. The connection with population is that all living beings are interconnected and when one species threatens the whole system—as human overpopulation is now threatening the earth—then nature tries to restore balance. Historically, disease, pandemics and plagues were the most effective ways of re-establishing stability.

In a sense, from a human perspective, we have been lucky with COVID-19. While highly infectious and with over four million deaths worldwide at the time of writing, fortunately COVID-19 is different to its viral predecessor, SARS-CoV (severe acute respiratory syndrome) which emerged in 2003. SARS had a low infection rate, but a high mortality rate of around 10%. If it had been as infectious as COVID-19, particularly the Delta variant, the death rate would have been much higher.

Pandemics are not new to humankind; they have always been with us, and recur on a semi-regular basis. Part of the reason for this is because there is a sense in which we are an exotic species across the world. Our original home is the region where we first evolved, the hot, moist climate of equatorial East Africa. Here tropical diseases and parasites kept human numbers low. But as we spread across the earth into different environments, our numbers increased. But every environment has a limit and as population increases and carrying-capacity is exceeded, resources begin run out and biodiversity decreases. There is a price to be paid for over-exploitation. Pathogens regularly emerge against which we have little or no resistance and people die.

Population size and pandemics are intimately linked, because historically disease has been a way of restoring the balance between human numbers and the demands we make on the natural world. With world overpopulation currently making such a massive impact on the earth through resource depletion, biodiversity loss and global warming, it is inevitable that some form of balance between humankind and the natural world needs to be restored. You don't have to be a philosopher to understand that the earth is a finite reality that cannot produce an infinite supply of resources for an ever-growing human population, yet our economic system is posited precisely on the possibility of unending growth. As David Attenborough bluntly says if we don't limit numbers 'we will starve'.

This book is based on the conviction that to save the planet we have to reduce our present numbers rapidly and that to achieve this we will have to adopt a radically new ethical approach. That's why I entitled it *The Depopulation Imperative*. I am simply trying to highlight the massive problem we face with so many people on earth. Sure, based on an optimistic assessment, human numbers will probably stabilize and then slowly begin to decrease somewhere between 2050 and 2100, but that maybe too late.

Given our present consumption patterns, we don't have time to wait several decades for something that we hope might happen. We have already seriously reduced and compromised biodiversity and destroyed vast swathes of the natural world. Our present resource use is far beyond sustainability. While pandemics are often the stuff of science fiction, there is every chance that a really catastrophic pandemic that really wipes out millions of people can and will occur at any time. There is a sense in which COVID-19 might be just a warning shot of what lies ahead.

At least we have some knowledge of how this disease originated. SARS-CoV-2 or COVID-19, like its predecessors SARS-CoV and MERS-CoV, are zoonotic diseases that crossed most probably from bats to humans via an animal intermediary. The natural hosts of SARS are horseshoe bats and it probably crossed to humans via cat-like civets, that are sold for food in so-called 'wet markets' in China and elsewhere in Asia. COVID-19 probably has the same origin and spread to humans via an as-yet unidentified intermediary animal, possibly pangolins, a small scaled mammal, known as 'the scaly anteater', prized in Chinese medicine for its scales and also its meat. It used to be common in Asia and sub-Saharan Africa, but its numbers have been decimated by the illegal wildlife trade.

However, the really unknown factor facing us in terms of infectious diseases are the long-term consequences of global warming. We already know that a 2.5° Celsius or greater increase in temperature will vastly extend the range of disease-carrying mosquitos that spread malaria, dengue fever, yellow fever, the Zika virus, West Nile virus and chikungunya (viral fever) which even now kill a million or more people each year. With an increase in mosquito numbers and range, we can expect a much higher fatality rate.

As human beings, we often delude ourselves. There are still many who claim that overpopulation is not a problem, that somehow a finite earth has no limits. All types of panaceas are suggested: technology, artificial intelligence, bio-engineering, genetically engineered food, life on the moon or other planets, to name a few. What is significant is that all of these artificial processes involve major interference in nature. All are the product of the seemingly incurable human obsession with manipulating our surroundings. I will deal with all of these issues in the book. But what we can't deny are the statistical facts: in 10,000BC there were about four million people on earth. Just after 1800AD, we crossed the one billion mark and by 1960 there were three billion. In July 2021 it was 7.9 billion. By 2050 the projected number is 9.8 billion. The destruction and havoc that this number will cause to the natural world and biodiversity is horrendous.

The sudden closing down of the world's economic system due to COVID-19 has given us a rare opportunity to reflect on what we're doing to the earth and to re-think some basic assumptions about what is important for us as individuals and societies. At least the virus has forced us to listen to and respect experts in epidemiology, virology and medicine and somewhat silenced the economic and business 'experts' who endlessly call for 'growth' in a finite world. What we need to do is to pause and resist the temptation to rush back to 'business as usual'. There is a sense in which we are gifted with this time to reassess our values and what is most important to us as human beings.

While it is vitally important to get the virus under control and for us to try to maintain a basic standard of living as we emerge from the virus, a whole other approach is necessary to begin rebuilding society. COVID-19 has given us an extraordinary chance to reflect on the bigger picture and to evolve alternative ways of thinking about and living in society. We have to resist the tendency to want to get back to economic 'normality' as quickly as possible, because developed countries have run-up enormous debt in the process of helping people through the shut-down.

Understandably people want to get back to 'normality' as quickly as possible, but my argument is that we need to pause precisely because COVID-19 is a symptom of something much bigger. And that larger context is that humankind's out-of-control numbers are in a dysfunctional relationship with the natural world as we demand more than the limited resources the earth can provide.

While this may be anathema to politicians whose visions are short-term because of the necessity of re-election, the closing-down of our economy by COVID-19 has given us a chance to pause and ask: what is the most important issue we face? The answer is that there are just too many people consuming too much; that we are far-exceeding the regenerative capacity of the earth. To deal with this we are going to have to shift from prioritizing ourselves to putting the natural world first. This will require a whole new ethical principle: the integrity and good of the earth must take priority over everything including our needs and desires.

While the book focuses on overpopulation, a whole range of other fundamental issues are embedded in this discussion. I will refer to them as I go along and will try to draw things together in a final chapter, as we look forward to the kind of world a sustainable population and a just, equitable society might look like after COVID-19. To begin let us examine a country where we can see the catastrophic effects of overpopulation in miniature.

I

A Country in Trouble

The highest fertility in the world

The land-locked West African country of Niger is named after the Niger River which rises in the Loma Mountains in eastern Sierra Leone and south-eastern Guinea. It flows north through Mali passing the legendary city of Timbuktu, then turns south through south-western Niger and flows on into Nigeria, eventually reaching the Atlantic at the Gulf of Guinea. The river is the lifeline of landlocked Niger, which became part of French West Africa in the early twentieth century. With a post-colonial history of political instability and military coups after independence in 1960, Niger is a very dangerous country with high levels of crime, armed robbery, kidnapping of foreigners and an increasing terrorist threat, even in the capital Niamey (population 774,000). However, on 27 December 2020 a reasonably peaceful democratic election took place leading to a run-off election in late-February 2021. This will be the first time an elected president will be succeeded by another elected president, despite attempts by terrorist groups to torpedo the democratic process.

Most of the country is situated in the Sahel region, the transition zone between the Sahara Desert to the north and the more fertile savanna and tropical regions to the south. The Sahel reaches across Africa from the Atlantic to the Red Sea. Parts of Niger are beautiful, especially the Aïr Mountains north of Agadez in the heart of Tuareg territory, the Sahara dwelling Berber people.

Niger is surrounded by Algeria and an unstable Libya to the north, Chad to the east, Nigeria and Benin to the south and Burkina-Faso and Mali to the west. Niger, which is about the size of France, is mainly desert, with just the southern two per cent of the land surface forests and woodland. While Niger's political leadership has been stable since early-2016, the whole Sahel region is very volatile with Islamist groups like Boko Haram, an al-Qaeda off-shoot, active on Niger's border with Nigeria, as well as in Burkina-Faso and Mali. These groups did their best to undermine the December 2020 election. Former Gaddafi loyalists from Libya are active in the northern Sahara region, leading to widespread brigandage. There are about 250,000 refugees in Niger, mostly from Nigeria.

With about 7% of the world's supply in northern Niger around the town of Arlit, the country's main export is uranium, making-up about 70% of its foreign trade. This, together with continuing political and social instability across the Sahel region, has led to increasing great power intervention by American special forces, as well as French, German, Canadian and Italian troops.[1] Boko Haram entered Niger from Mali and is active in the uranium mining area in the arid center of the country. In addition to security problems, the largely French owned uranium mining operation is leading to environmental health problems that are impacting local children, largely as a result of exposure to radiation. In fact, the country is gaining little from its uranium exports.

With about 3.5 million people in 1960, Niger's mid-2021 population was 25.1 million. It has one of the fastest population growth rates—the number of births over deaths—in the world at 3.9% annually, with a fertility rate in 2021 of 6.95 children per woman, the world's highest. Estimates have the population reaching around 60 million or more by 2050, a totally unsustainable number. Contraceptives are freely available, but usage is low and with a median age of fifteen, the prognosis for effective population control is minimal.

Niger is geographically West Africa's largest country, but 95% of the population live a poor, rural lifestyle on the one third of arable and semi-arable land in the south, where the capital Niamey is situated. The country suffers from recurrent natural crises, especially droughts and locust infestations. The soil is superficial and low in nutrients; overgrazing is common. Firewood is used by everyone for cooking, leading to widespread deforestation. The per capita annual income is about US$420, with 60% of the population living on less than a dollar a day. Life expectancy is 60.4 years. Neighbouring countries have lower life expectancies: Chad is 52.9 years, Nigeria 53.4 and Mali 57.9. Niger is the poorest country in the world according the UN's 2018 Human Development Index, a tool that measures life expectancy, education and per capita income.

Social, religious and family dynamics and the fact that Niger has not ratified the Maputo Protocol which guarantees the right of women to decide when to have children, the number they will have and the spacing of their pregnancies, means that women and girls lack the freedom to control childbearing. More than half of girls are married before they are fifteen and many eighteen-year-olds already have four or five children. Polygamy is legal and common, with many men having multiple wives. There is enormous social pressure on women from their husbands, families and in-laws to have more children, because fertility is seen as a sign of wealth and power. As a result, fertility is highly valued and both men and women say they want more children. Mortality among women is high with them facing a one-in-twenty-three chance of dying from pregnancy or childbirth. Girls don't get the chance to finish primary school with an 11% literacy rate for females; the general adult literacy rate is 19%, the second lowest in the world. Only one in five children enter secondary school.

The key population problem is persuading and educating both men and women to have fewer children, and then providing the means to limit family size. Decisions about a woman's fertility are often made by their husbands, so both sexes have to be persuaded to limit fertility, especially given the strong social pressure to have more children. With such a young age of marriage, the resulting impact on girls and women is horrendous. In this context family planning is not so much about preventing pregnancy, as trying to make space between children to give women a chance to recover and care for the children they already have. Incursions by Boko Haram attacking schools, killing teachers, kidnapping young women and forcing girls back to their villages have exacerbated fears of sending girls to school. The situation is being further degraded by climate change which is contracting the productive area of the country.

Influence of Islam

Niger's Muslim community, which makes-up 97% of the population, is a complex mixture. It is traditionally Sunni, mixed with a strong Sufi strain that has a long history of being tolerant of a syncretistic amalgam of Islam with animist beliefs and practices. However, in the last two decades a more fundamentalist strain of Islam has been replacing the more tolerant Sufism, with the increasing influence of Boko Haram and the return of young people from study in the Gulf states. Extreme Islamists, in contrast to moderate Islam, encourage high rates of fertility and put pressure on men to force their wives to have as many children as possible.

The key to stabilizing the situation is bringing population growth under control and then reducing it. But the socio-familial grip of high fertility makes this extremely difficult. Pregnancy and forty days of caring for a young infant at least give girls a break from hard physical labour. As one woman says, babies 'come with two hands to work, but only one mouth to feed'. Another says 'I like to make the Muslim community grow'.[2] All experts agree that the only solution is the education and liberation of girls and women. In that context, Niger leaves you with a feeling of despair about rampant population growth and low educational and living standards.

But Niger's problems are symptomatic of the kind of problems that are widespread in Africa. In mid-2021 the continent accounted for 1.37 billion people with a median age of 19.4 years. In 2050 the estimated Africa-wide population will be 2.2 billion. This is more than half of the estimated global population increase for that thirty-year period. Niger and similar countries in the same region are caught in a vicious circle: the fundamental social mores of the culture, justified by a religious overlay, deprives people, particularly women, of education and keeps them in poverty leading to early marriage, large families and an ever-growing population, which re-enforces the ignorance and poverty that created the problem in the first place. The only way of dealing with this is to attempt to persuade both men and women that education, especially of girls, can create other opportunities beyond endless fertility. Boys and men also need education about the close connection between population and poverty. We already know that the education of women and the creation of opportunities for them beyond childbearing works, but the solution has to come from the bottom up, supported by international aid.

But, having said that, I'm tempted to say that in a situation like Niger—and more generally in Africa—we're whistling in the wind. While laudable efforts are being made, particularly with the education of girls, the time-frame for controlling and reducing population is so short and the challenges so great that perhaps the only solution is for things to be allowed to work themselves out, painful and disastrous as that will be for those who will have to live through it. But at least it respects the social conditioning that these people have inherited and embraced. Perhaps only sad experience will teach them that high rates of fertility don't work and ultimately lead to disaster.

2

'Don't mention population'

A fundamental principle

While Niger is the future of Africa in microcosm, experience has taught me that tackling population head-on, let alone *de*population, might win you a few supporters, while risking the alienation of many. That's why shrewd politicians run for cover when asked for their views on population. It's like Basil Fawlty and the war; only the 'brave', or the foolhardy publicly comment on it. Sure, most informed people generally agree that we have a 'population problem', but they see it as someone else's issue. It's an Asian, African, or developing world predicament, not one that concerns them. Nevertheless, people still have strong opinions. Once you get down to details as to whether the world is over-populated, or what we're going to do about it, hackles rise, even among those who are aware of the serious ecological and environmental challenges we're facing.

Many people resist discussing population precisely because this is an issue that touches us all intimately, yet seems insoluble. It throws up moral and religious conundrums about family size and the right to have children, it confronts us with the role of the community and the state in determining the number of children that couples have, it asks questions about sustainable population and about whether even developed countries are over-populated. It touches on deeply-held spiritual convictions, on basic issues of social justice and the massive inequalities in distribution between the poor and the rich, both within Western societies themselves, and between the developed and developing worlds. It impacts on our deeply held anthropocentrism, the assumption that we come first before every other species. The underlying, usually unconscious presumption is that we must prioritize the needs of humanity first over all other species and the natural world. The extraordinary irony is that given we make-up just 0.01% of all living things, the notion that we somehow constitute the entire meaning of the world, let alone the cosmos, is outrageously presumptuous.

Martin Luther King, who had strong views on family planning, was right when he said back in 1966 that 'the modern plague of overpopulation is soluble by means we have discovered and with resources we possess'. But he added that 'What is lacking is ... [a] universal consciousness of the gravity of the problem and education of the billions who are its victims.'[3] Sir David Attenborough was equally direct when he asked 'how will we feed this enormous horde?'[4] However, despite King and Attenborough, overpopulation is one of those realities that just doesn't fit into the individualistic, post-modern *zeitgeist*. We seem to find it extraordinarily difficult to face-up to complex issues like this. Nevertheless, this is precisely what this book attempts to do.

Right up-front, I confess that I'm convinced that we need an entirely new foundational moral principle to guide us, one that prioritizes the earth and biodiversity. I'm unequivocally saying that the natural world and the survival of other species takes priority over absolutely everything, including the desires, needs and even the welfare of individual human persons and communities. There is no middle position here, no compromise to make this principle more palatable. Even for our own survival, this principle must be accepted as normative for all moral and ethical action. Otherwise, the future is going to be very bleak, even for people alive today, let alone our grandchildren.

A fundamental moral issue here centres around the ethics involved in inter-generational rights: what are our moral responsibilities if we consume resources and degrade the earth so that the quality of life of future generations is deeply compromised? If we continue the way we're going then, as I said in my 1995 book *God's Earth*, we may become 'the most despised and cursed generations in the history of humankind ... because without regard for the future we have rendered the earth less and less inhabitable'.[5] Never before has the earth been so exploited and degraded and biodiversity so devastated.

The principle of earth first is profoundly subversive because it directly undermines the individualistic anthropocentrism which unconsciously dominates our presuppositions and decisions. The word 'anthropocentrism' needs some explanation. It assumes that humankind constitutes the essential purpose and meaning of the world and even the cosmos itself. Derived from the Greek word Ανθρωποσ ('anthropos') meaning 'humankind' in the generic sense, it centres the whole meaning of reality on and in us. In religious terms it embraces the notion that the world was created by God primarily for humankind and that human life alone has absolute value. All other species have relative value, an importance that is often only seen in relationship to us. From a secular perspective, anthropocentrism signifies that we constitute the ultimate meaning of evolution and that all other species and the world's resources are subservient to us and our needs and can be exploited by us as required.

A related word that has come into contemporary usage is 'Anthropocene'. This word is posited on the assumption that the changes that are currently occurring as a result of human impacts on the world's ecosystems are so monumental that many believe that we are entering a new geological era that requires a new word to describe it. Geologically speaking, we are still in the Holocene epoch, meaning 'very recent', but the word Anthropocene seems to have gained widespread currency and has become the accepted scientific nomenclature for our age.

Cynics and even sympathetic readers will say that if I think we're going to abandon anthropocentrism, then I'm living in unreality! If I think that people in the backblocks of Niger, or on drowning Pacific atolls, let alone those in high rise apartments in Manhattan, or in Indian slums, or coal mining towns in Australia, are suddenly going to abandon anthropocentrism and put the earth and biocentrism first, then I'm living in fantasy-land. Perhaps, but I also think that the consequences of global warming, biodiversity loss and a rapid decline in the natural world will force people to re-assess anthropocentrism and move toward a more earth-centric stance. What I want to achieve in this book is to provide a moral principle that will guide our practical judgments about these issues.

Something else that might help to change human attitudes is COVID-19. Because it de-stabilizes us, questions our certainties and makes us vulnerable, Coronavirus gives us a chance to re-examine deep-seated issues that we assume are irrefutable, like much of contemporary economic theory underpinning neo-liberal, free market capitalism linked to endless consumption and 'infinite' growth in a finite world. As George Monbiot has said, most people have no idea that neo-liberalism is the ideology that dominates our lives. They simply see it as the way the economy works, the way things have always been. 'So pervasive has neo-liberalism become that we seldom even recognise it as an ideology. We appear to accept the proposition that this utopian, millenarian faith describes a neutral force; a kind of biological law … But [this] philosophy arose as a conscious attempt to reshape human life and shift the locus of power' away from the community and representative government, to businesses and corporations.[6] It is, in fact, a secular religion.

Pandemics shake our certainties about what we think are unchangeable beliefs and force us back to the moral basics. Another long-term lesson from COVID-19 is that it confronts us with the fact that our lives are rooted in the biological structure of the world, that we are not separate from and over against nature, but an intimate part of it. We need to develop a sense of seeing ourselves as part of the world, rather than seeing nature as something separate from us that we can use and abuse as we wish. Perhaps the most important lesson of COVID-19 is that it reminds us of our sheer impermanence and vulnerability.

Despite the fact that it will infuriate some people, an uncompromising emphasis on the priority of earth first must become our core moral principle. The preservation of the wonderful biological diversity of life, expressed in all its detail and species, together with the maintenance of the integrity of the earth, must come before everything else. And by 'everything' I mean everything, including us. Our lives and needs are not absolute, but relative to the good of the whole. We are rooted in the earth's biological system and are utterly dependent upon it. We don't, and never have constituted the ultimate meaning of the planet, let alone the cosmos. We have no over-riding right to dominate the world, or destructively exploit it. Individual human lives and particular human communities are relative to the whole and must act within the context of the good of the entire earth community. Given our total dependence on the earth system, to think or act otherwise is delusional. I will return to this fundamental principle later; here I simply state it, so you know where I stand and where my argument is going.

Reducing population numbers

As we will see in the next chapter, human population numbers have been growing since *homo sapiens* first emerged. But the real escalation in numbers began just after 1800. In the 120 years since 1900, world population has increased from 1.62 billion to 7.9 billion as the following table illustrates:

	1700	1800	1900	1975	2000	2020	2030	2050
Europe	120m	180m	390m	635m	710m	747m	741m	710m
Asia	370m	625m	970m	2.3b	3.5b	4.6b	5.0b	5.29b
Africa	61m	70m	110m	385m	700m	1.3b	1.69b	2.49b
Americas	13m	24m	145m	545m	815m	1.02b	1.9b	1.18b
Oceania	2m	2m	7m	23m	36m	42m	48m	57m
TOTALS	566m	899m	1.62b	3.88b	5.76b	7.8b	8.55b	9.74b

The challenge we face today is not just a matter of stabilizing population numbers at or slightly below Zero Population Growth (ZPG) by 2050, but a significant reduction in *present* population numbers. This is an essential precondition for the preservation of what has not already been destroyed or consumed. Unless the issue of the *reduction* of human numbers is tackled, all our efforts at environmental remediation will be useless. This is an enormous moral challenge and we have so little time left in which to do it. If we don't tackle this right now, the near future will be very bleak indeed and it is hard to see human civilization and culture surviving. We owe it to our children and grandchildren to act decisively now. Otherwise, as someone said, 'all that will remain is to negotiate the precise terms of our extinction'. And we might not even get a chance to do that! I know that such rhetoric sounds apocalyptic, or to use the modern jargon word 'catastrophist', and that catastrophe is often the refuge of madmen. But the overpopulation crisis and the pressure that we're putting on the life-systems of the planet and on other species, in fact fulfils the description of a genuine catastrophe. Historically we have never been in this situation before and the old solutions no longer work. Humanity is in dire trouble and the only way out is for us to act in an entirely different way. We don't have another choice.

Flowing from my basic principle, there are two general arguments that underpin this book. The first confronts facts and statistics, the reality of the world in which we live. By any rational estimate there are already far too many of us and while globally our absolute numbers are slowing down, it's not a matter of reaching some form of equilibrium in the mid-distant future, but of decreasing our numbers now back to a level where we are less of a problematic species. We already live in a world of over-exploited resources with us asset-stripping and heating the oceans, degrading whole landscapes and seriously changing weather patterns by our use of carbon-based fuels like oil, coal and gas.

Linked to this is the reality that everything in the natural world is interconnected; if you interfere with one element there will be flow-on effects to others. For example, burning fossil fuels leads to global warming and widespread landscape fires, which in turn leads to ice melt in the Arctic, Antarctic, Greenland and the world's glaciers, resulting in sea level rises, flooding and the loss of whole coastal regions that are home sometimes to millions of people. An example is the Ganges-Brahmaputra Delta in Bangladesh and India. Displaced, these people then become environmental refugees looking for somewhere else to live. We should have left the coal, oil and gas in the ground in the first place.

If we accept the fundamental moral principle that prioritizes the earth and biodiversity, then we have to question whether the assumption that human needs and preferences must always come first. We are primarily responsible for environmental destruction resulting in massive species loss, as well as global warming. Sure, in historical terms we have always had an impact on the earth, but in the past our smaller numbers meant that this was limited, although the destructiveness of our human ancestors moving into pristine environments should not be under-estimated. But nowadays our numbers are out of all proportion, resulting in an environmental catastrophe. That's why it's not just a matter of stabilizing population, but of reducing our numbers to stop the on-going damage that 7.9 billion people are already wreaking on the earth. To reach population stability, fertility must remain at 2.1 children per woman. Above that, population rises; below it, population falls. The population of developed countries is already decreasing, with increases coming from immigration. For example, the 2017 figure for the European Union was 1.59 children per woman. France had the highest fertility rate with 1.90 births per woman and Malta the lowest at 1.26.

But the problem is that these figures are not reflected worldwide. It will be 2050 or later before many middle-sized developing countries like Mexico, Algeria, Turkey and Peru reach a stable 2.1 children per woman. In the forty-eight poorest and least developed countries, thirty-two of which are in Africa, this stabilized figure won't be reached until very late this century, or perhaps not until the early-2100s, if then. Countries with a fertility rate in 2021 like Niger (6.95), Mali (6.26), and Angola (6.16) top the list, but there are eleven other countries with fertility rates above five. All, except Afghanistan, are in Africa. There the population will jump to an estimated 2.49 billion in 2050, despite the impact of AIDS, tuberculosis, Coronavirus and other factors reducing the population.

There is vigorous and oftentimes hostile debate about how we tackle depopulation. The basic spectrum of opinion ranges from Malthusian pessimism to naturalistic optimism. The pessimists, following Thomas Malthus – more on him later – believe that the population problem is intractable and will only be solved by measures like limiting fertility and making sterilization and abortion widely available. The optimists contend that humanity is very adaptable and that population equilibrium will be reached through free market capitalism without regulatory intervention. Some Malthusians favor coercive, compulsory limitations on reproduction, legally enforced by governments, whereby individual fertility is limited through contraception, sterilization and abortion, as happened in China and

India. The most obvious problem with the coercive approach is that it tends to see the whole issue from a single causal perspective: cut back population by whatever means necessary, and our environmental problems will end. The evidence points to a more complex situation.

This approach is opposed by those with a strong emphasis on human dignity and rights and by religious people with moral concerns about using such means to limit reproduction. This approach believes that priority must be given to social and distributive justice. This is the mainstream Christian approach. The argument is that the obvious imbalance between the living standards of the developed world and the twenty or more per cent of people who are starving, or seriously under-nourished, is scandalous. From this social justice and equity perspective, the imbalance creates an ethical demand that developed countries lower their standard of living and share their wealth with countries in need. They also argue that there is a basic ethical right, overriding the powers of nation states, to allow migration from countries of overpopulation and chronic shortage, to those with apparent space and surplus food. However, on its own, the social justice approach is ineffective in stemming population growth, let alone protecting the environment. The emphasis here is not so much on ecology and biodiversity, as on human-focused equity; it is embedded in an anthropocentric view that justice for all comes before everything else. A better environment and a lower population are, at best, by-products.

But where social justice advocates are right is when they insist on the necessity of reducing economic growth and lowering the expectations that people have of unsustainable standards of living in both the developed and developing world. But how do you persuade people in the West to lower their standards of living and how do you set limits to the expectations of those in developing countries? Given that the world population is expected to stabilize by 2050 and that it is already dropping in the developed world, it would achieve nothing if people in emerging economies expected to live at the same level as contemporary Westerners. Yet that is what the burgeoning middle classes in countries like China and India demand as their expenditure moves from basic needs to wants and luxuries. The fact is that expectations will have to be trimmed by both Westerners and the emerging middle class in developing countries. This is based on the recognition that the earth is finite and that we cannot continue to produce and consume resources at the present rate.

Another contribution to overpopulation is increasing life expectancy. With better medical care, people are living longer. For instance, the number of people globally aged sixty and over is predicted to increase from 962 million in 2017 to 2.1 billion in 2050. According to Max Roser 'life expectancy has increased from less than 30 years [in 1800] to over 72 years now; after two centuries of progress, we can expect to live more than twice as long as our ancestors. And this progress was … achieved in … every world region.'[7] This is true even of Africa where an increase in life expectancy has been driven mainly by improvements in child survival and expanded access to antiretrovirals for the treatment of HIV.

But there is a sense in which there is nothing new in our current dilemma. Incurably manipulative, *Homo sapiens* has a long history of exploiting biodiversity, consuming the future and eventually destroying the very landscape upon which human survival depends.

3

The Ambivalent Story of
Homo sapiens

Human destructiveness

Humankind has a long history of catastrophic behaviour on moving into new and pristine environments. First, I will examine some scenarios from recent history showing how devastating modern Europeans have been when they moved into new regions.

The first example comes from Hobart in the Australian island state of Tasmania. The city is situated on the estuary of the Derwent River, directly beneath the magnificent 1271 metre (4170 feet) high Mount Wellington. There is much that is still unique about Tasmania, especially its flora and fauna. Almost equal in size to the Republic of Ireland, Tasmania was cut-off from south-eastern Australia at the end of the last ice age, about 12,000YBP. The island then evolved in isolation. It was in Hobart in early-September 1936 that a unique animal became extinct.

British settlement in 1803 shattered the island's isolation and the Aboriginal population, numbering between 4000 and 6000 people, was almost destroyed in what is now seen as a genocide. Many of the unique fauna were also decimated, among them thylacine (*Thylacinus cynocephalus*), a dog-headed, carnivorous marsupial, that is an animal in which the young are born prematurely and nurtured in a pouch below the mother's belly. Thylacine was yellowish-brown to grey in colour with fifteen to twenty distinct dark stripes across its back. In size and appearance, it looked like a large dog and even had a kind of bark. It occupied a similar ecological niche to dogs and wolves. It had survived in Tasmania, but had been extinct on the Australian mainland for 3000 years.

Variously called by the early European settlers the 'Tasmanian tiger' (from the stripes on its back), 'marsupial wolf', 'native hyaena' and even 'panther', the names given to thylacine are significant. 'The sad fact is the animal attracted names of opprobrium from human forces increasingly opposed to its existence.'[8] The problem for thylacine was that sheep and fine wool production quickly became important in the Tasmanian economy and the animal was blamed for predation on sheep and chickens, even though this was nothing more than a confected rural myth. In fact, thylacine was a rare predator on sheep, but a vociferous farming lobby pressured successive nineteenth and early-twentieth century Tasmanian governments to place a bounty on thylacines. Hunting the Tasmanian tiger became a 'sport' in the bush. The animal, like the local Aborigines, was seen as representing of a lower form of life that was not worth preserving. Hunting was so effective that we can date exactly the death of the last known living thylacine, a female. It died in Beaumaris Zoo on Queens Domain near the center of Hobart on the night of 7 September 1936. These extraordinary animals, the product of 160 million years of evolution, had been driven to extinction by wilful human stupidity. Thylacine researcher, Robert Paddle says that sadly 'there is nothing unique about the history of the destruction of the thylacine … predictable and disturbing parallels in the treatment of indigenous carnivores may be found almost at will in the invasive history of human colonization over the past millennium.' Paddle adds that scientists 'proved pathetically ineffective in countering such destruction'.[9]

We can also date exactly the extinction of a North American bird. On 1 September 1914 the last passenger pigeon (*Ectopistes migratorius*) died in Cincinnati Zoo. The passenger pigeon was a fast-moving, migratory bird, native to eastern and midwestern North America. It is estimated there were three to five billion passenger pigeons in North America at the time of European settlement in the early-seventeenth century. There were so many that the possibility of their extinction seemed unimaginable. They lived and moved in vast flocks that often numbered in the millions and their sheer numbers protected them. Their migrations in search of nesting sites and food 'took hours to pass over a single spot, darkening the firmament and making normal conversation inaudible'.[10] They lived on acorns, beechnuts, strawberries, figs and blueberries and were often destructive of crops. They were sustainably hunted by native Americans in spring as a source of protein after winter. But as the European population of North America increased – up from 3.9 million in 1790, the year of the first US census, to seventy-six million by 1900 – passenger pigeons became a cheap source of food, especially for the poor. After the Civil War (1861–1865), hunting them became a commercial industry 'fuelled by professional sportsmen who could learn quickly about new nestings and follow the flocks around the continent', through the telegraph and the railroad.[11] The birds were killed by shooting, net trapping, asphyxiation with burning sulphur, or attacking them with rakes and pitchforks. It was reported that in the post-Civil War period, 50,000 birds per day were killed in Michigan alone. They might have survived if their nesting sites had not been raided to harvest the young birds. Even as their numbers crashed in the late-nineteenth century, no effort was made to save them and the species became extinct in 1914.

At the same time another North American near-extinction scenario was occurring. With the completion of the trans-continental railroad in May 1869, open season was declared on the vast herds of millions of bison that roamed the great plains west of the Mississippi and east of the Rockies. The killing was supported by the US government after the Civil War, because they were determined to bring the Native American peoples of the plains to heel, and they depended on the bison as a food supply. As a result, 'the lives of countless Native Americans were destroyed, and tens of millions of bison, which had roamed freely upon the Great Plains since the last ice age 10,000 years ago, were nearly driven to extinction in a massive slaughter made possible by the railroad.'[12] The animals were shot from slow-moving trains by 'sportsmen' armed with high-powered rifles. By the end of the nineteenth century only three hundred bison were left in the wild. The number has revived to two hundred thousand today.

In Australia in the late-nineteenth century a similar decimation of an iconic marsupial, the koala, occurred as the animals were killed, often cruelly, to supply fur for the fashion industry. As recent as August 1927 the Queensland state government declared 'open season' on koalas and 600,000 pelts were collected and an estimated 800,000 were killed. Not surprisingly, koalas are now listed in that state as 'vulnerable'.

These scenarios stand as modern symbols of the voracious stupidity of the ironically named *homo sapiens sapiens*, literally 'wise, wise person'; *sapiens* in Latin means 'wise', 'knowing', 'sensible, or 'well advised'. To describe humankind as environmentally *sapiens* is highly questionable, given our ever-expanding numbers, ravenous appetites and rampant destructiveness. But such behaviour goes right back to our ancestors and Harvard socio-biologist, Edward O. Wilson is correct when he describes humankind as 'a serial killer of the biosphere', especially in pristine environments where the arrival of humans has been disastrous for other species. He says that 'first to go among animal species are the big, the slow and the tasty', the megafauna. 'Also doomed were a substantial fraction of the most easily captured ground birds and tortoises.'[13] Wilson cites New Zealand as a prime example. It was the world's last uninhabited land mass when a small group of Polynesians arrived, possibly from the Cook, Society, or Marquesas Islands, sometime around 950AD. The first settlers discovered an absolute wonderland teeming with food sources, including several species of moa, a large flightless bird. Then, 'like a sweep of the scythe', the moa was gone.[14] The colonists had inadvertently brought rats that attacked smaller birds, reptiles and amphibians, while burning and clearing soon reduced habitats to marginal levels. Historian John Man, commenting specifically on New Zealand, says that politically correct 'urbanized romantics' idealize 'hunter-gatherers as embodiments of ecological wisdom carefully preserving their food sources from overuse'. He says that 'it is hard to find evidence to support this belief'.[15] Australian biologist, Tim Flannery simply calls us 'future eaters'.[16] Undoubtedly, we are the greatest threat to biodiversity.

Humankind and biodiversity

Why is biodiversity important? Fundamentally because it supports all life on earth, including ours. In fact, forty per cent of the world's economy is derived from biological sources which provide basic natural services for our very survival as a species. More than that, it adds to the rich, magnificent and beautiful diversity of life.

Since the advent of humankind almost all extinction scenarios are attributable, either directly or indirectly, to our pressure on ecosystems and the way in which we use landscapes. This is because we are, from an ecosystem point of view, an exotic species, divorced from our natural environment. Our unique ecological niche is in equatorial East Africa where diseases and pathogens that are endemic in the area kept our ancestors' numbers in check. The *Australopithecines*, the first hominids, evolved in the Great Rift Valley in present-day East Africa, stretching through Ethiopia, Kenya, Uganda and Tanzania. There they passed through a five million year-long, complex, non-linear developmental process that eventually produced our near ancestor *Homo habilis*, who eventually evolved into *Homo erectus*, with an overlap between them of about half a million years. About 190,000 years ybp *Homo sapiens* probably evolved from *erectus*. After such a long history it is clear that humankind's ancestral home is East Africa and that in other landscapes, we are an exotic species.

There are two main theories as to how humans spread across the world. One is that *Homo erectus* left Africa about a million years ago, evolving into *sapiens* in several regions. The other is that a group of already evolved *sapiens* left Africa to spread out over Europe and Asia. Whichever theory is right, 'the enormous evolutionary potential pent up in the populations of *Homo erectus* generated a dynamic state of biological development toward the *sapiens* state'.[17] As humans adapted to cooler, less tropical climates, numbers increased because of the absence of East African pathogens. Human entry into pristine environments would have also provided our ancestors with abundant food sources, thus enhancing population numbers.

Sapiens' greater brain capacity meant that humans could transmit high level knowledge and skills down generations and develop a sense of continuity and culture. All animals can transmit knowledge to their offspring, but humankind has developed this into a complex cultural process that surpasses other species. Epidemiologist, Tony McMichael, points out that this has allowed 'successive generations to start progressively further along the road of cultural and technological development. By traveling that road, the human species has … become

19

increasingly distanced from its ecological roots.'[18] This has allowed humans to expand their ability to exploit resources and maintain higher populations. But particular ecological niches also set limits to carrying capacity, especially when resources were exhausted. Population increases are achieved 'at the cost of reductions in biodiversity' and they always run the danger of over-exploiting their environments, leading to the collapse of the offending civilization. 'It is in the nature of ecological systems that debts are finally called in,' McMichael says.[19] The point here is that once out of East Africa, humans manipulated their environment to suit their own needs and, in the process, brought about the extinction of other species through their interventions.

The New Zealand case is a relatively modern example of a series of mass extinctions perpetrated by humankind. The earliest examples of this occurred when our ancestors, the hunter-gatherers, began arriving in pristine Late-Pleistocene environments from about 65,000–70,000ybp. They targeted the large vertebrates, the megafauna like the woolly mammoths and mastodons of the northern hemisphere and the giant wombats and kangaroos of Australia. Systematic hunting began as a by-product of the development of language, the evolution of cultural intentionality, or sense of purpose, and the expansion of the use of flints and arrowheads. When people first penetrated pristine regions they hunted the megafauna because they were easy, slow-moving targets, eventually eliminating them.

This is what palaeontologist Paul Martin, discussing the North American context, calls the 'overkill hypothesis'.[20] This is a fiercely debated thesis that in many ways is influenced by contemporary cultural attitudes towards indigenous peoples. Some argue that indigenous peoples and their ancestors have always been responsible custodians of nature; others maintain that ancient indigenous peoples were primarily responsible for Late-Pleistocene extinction scenarios as they took what they needed from the landscape with little understanding of the species they hunted. They only gradually learned through experience to live in co-existence with nature. Those who idealise the hunter-gatherers as environmental saints blame late-Pleistocene climate change for the extinction of the megafauna.

Australia is sometimes cited as an example of the overkill hypothesis, although this is contested. The argument is complicated by a series of very recent discoveries which keep pushing back the date of human arrival on the continent. Evidence from a site in Northern Australia indicates that the most recent arrival date is up to 65,000ybp. If this is correct then humans arrived in Australia some 18,000 years earlier than had been previously thought.[21] The megafauna (such as *Macropus gigantus* (giant kangaroo), *Diprotodon* (giant wombat) and *Thylacoleo carnifex* (marsupial carnivore)) disappeared somewhere around 45,000–43,000ybp. If this date is accurate, then it means that humans co-existed with the megafauna in Australia for some 20,000 years, thus seemingly absolving them of overkill. Proponents of this view claim that the Australian megafauna were finally eliminated by climate change.

However, the evidence can be interpreted differently to support a modified overkill thesis. The original argument was that human arrival in Australia broadly corresponded with the disappearance of the megafauna. But it's almost unbelievable that such a small group of humans could have had such a continent-wide impact so quickly. But if small groups of humans arrived in Australia some 20,000 years earlier, then they would have had time to multiply and spread across the immense landscape of Australia (more than 7.8 million square kilometres or three million square miles) hunting their way through the most accessible food. No one is claiming that the hunter-gatherers were killing on an industrial scale, like the bison or thylacine hunts. Linked to indigenous fire practices whereby large areas were burned, it is possible that a kind of imperceptible overkill occurred. This makes sense given the massive size of the continent, the small population of humans, and the diversity of landscapes and environments.

Those who claim that Australian megafauna were eliminated by climate change fail to consider that these large animals had survived many previous climate changes over millions of years of evolution without becoming extinct. Recent research in south-west Western Australia shows 'no indication … that the megafauna suffered a slow demise commensurate with increases in aridity'. Rather the argument is that these large animals 'are demographically vulnerable to hunting pressure owing to their typically low reproduction rates and low population growth', and conclude that 'it has been estimated that low intensity hunting … could result in a species being extinguished over a few hundred years'. This is what these researchers call 'imperceptible overkill'.[22]

Another example of imperceptible overkill is North America. While the date of human arrival is contested 'we can solidly say that people were across the Americas by 15,000 years ago … and there's enough evidence to suggest humans were widespread 20,000 years ago. There's [also] some evidence of people as far back as 30,000 to 40,000 years ago.'[23]As in Australia, there is debate around the role humans played in North American megafaunal extinction with some questioning the overkill hypothesis, claiming that climate change and environmental stresses led to their disappearance. But again, this contradicts the fact that these animals, like their Australian counterparts, had already survived many climate changes over millions of years. The only new element in the scenario was humankind and, while warming may have played some part, the imperceptible overkill scenario is as plausible in North America as it is in Australia. All the evidence is that humans, whether ancient or modern, are incurable manipulators of their environments, to the detriment of other species and the earth itself. However, as indigenous people worldwide demonstrate, humans can eventually achieve a balance with nature and live in a relatively sustainable way.

Increase of human population

Around 10,000ybp some hunter-gatherers in some places began to change. They began to focus on specific plants and animals that they could control and domesticate. An agricultural revolution began. In a remarkably quick transition between 10,000 and 8000ybp, some hunter-gatherers settled-down and began a life based on agriculture and the domestication of animals like sheep, cattle, goats and pigs. This seems to have happened first in the Fertile Crescent around the Tigris and Euphrates Rivers in south-eastern Turkey, Iraq and western Iran, with similar developments in the upper Nile region in Egypt. Around the same time people in China, parts of America, Africa and New Guinea also begun to domesticate animals and cultivate edible plants.[24] This period parallels the end of the most recent Ice Age which led to a warmer and more liveable environment with the evolution of temperate regions in the Middle East, China, southeast Asia and Central America.

Settlement led to clearing and cultivating pristine lands, stream diversions and irrigation. People later began using draught animals for ploughs and eventually for wheeled wagons. They destroyed any plants or animals that posed a threat to their way of life. While they still used stone tools, they began to settle down and coalesce into larger, more complex, permanent, hierarchical societies in villages, city states and eventually into larger, complex entities. Social classes began to emerge as people specialized and the development of art and language intensified. Rivalry over resources and power led to more sophisticated warfare.

Whatever the benefits for humankind, the transition to agriculture had disastrous environmental consequences. Hunter-gatherer groups were constantly on the move and never put too much pressure on any one landscape, whereas settled farming communities replaced natural landscapes with agricultural ones, throwing ecosystems out of balance, eventually destroying them. The present denuded-desert state of the misnamed 'Fertile Crescent' is testimony to the consequences of industrial scale agriculture. What happened was that excessive irrigation progressively increased the water table level with consequent salinity, gradually turning the whole region into the desert landscape of today. Given the widespread and often destructive contemporary use of irrigation throughout the world, it seems that *homo sapiens* is peculiarly obtuse in learning inconvenient truths from the past.

The long-term result of the Neolithic demographic transition, as this shift to settled agriculture is called, was a more stable, predictable existence and longer life spans, leading to population increases. This is the beginning of human population growth that lasted through until today. There were periodic downturns, but essentially up until 1800AD there has been a gradual increase in human numbers since 10,000ybp.

Of course, estimated human numbers for the past are, at best, informed guesses that can vary widely. However, historical demographers, Colin McEvedy and Richard Jones estimate that the worldwide hunter-gatherer population was perhaps around one million at the beginning of the last Ice Age (c.75,000ybp) when freezing conditions descended on what had been a reasonably habitable landscape for humans. But *homo sapiens* adapted to the cold and at the end of the last Ice Age the human numbers began to grow again, so that by 10,000 to 8000ybp they had probably reached around four million. Most of the earth was now populated, so 'further advance could only be achieved via higher densities'.[25]

The agricultural revolution had created the circumstances in which population could increase rapidly in a given region, preventing a return to the hunter-gatherer stage. For the first 5000 years of this revolution population growth was sluggish, because the area under cultivation was too small to support bigger numbers. The shift to agriculture was not a sudden transition; it was a slow, step-by-step process. Human numbers continued to increase slowly, but around 5000BC they began to accelerate. 'There was ... a gain of nearly 50% in the course of the fifth millennium BC and of roughly 100% in the course of the next three millennia.' With the coming of the iron age around 1000BC in Europe and the Near East, population growth exploded with numbers reaching 100 million by 500BC. 'Never before had there been so many people multiplying so fast.'[26]

Estimates for world population in the second century BC are around 150 million and by 200AD there were about 200 million people. This was the time of the Roman empire in the Mediterranean region and the Han empire in China. In terms of the Roman Empire, the peak population of about sixty-five million was in the early second century AD, especially during the reigns of Emperors Trajan (98–117) and Hadrian (117–138) when the empire reached its economic zenith. By the beginning of the fourth century population numbers had declined to about fifty-five million.

The other big population concentration was in Han China. Around 100AD it was about fifty-three million, and by 200AD it had risen to about sixty-three million. After that the population declined, so that by 400AD it had dropped back to fifty-three million.[27]

The third century AD marks a turning point both in the Mediterranean world and in China because the slave-dependent Roman and Han empires had both reached the limits of their technologies and their economies were increasingly unsustainable.

The Han dynasty collapsed in 220 followed by 350 years of civil war. By 300 the Roman Empire was becoming ungovernable, despite the administrative reforms of Emperor Diocletian (284–305). On the last day of 407AD the barbarian tribes crossed the frozen Rhine River in an invasion that Peter Brown calls 'a "gold rush" of immigrants'.[28] The western Roman empire collapsed. The European population fell to thirty-one million by 400AD and to twenty-six million by 600AD due to constant food shortages, recurrent plague, political instability and invasions by Vandals, Visigoths, Huns and later Vikings. In civil war-ridden China, it had dropped to fifty million by 600AD.[29] Human numbers in Africa, America and Oceania were also in decline.

In a way, the year 1000AD marks a turning point, because it is the moment when populations begin to increase again. In Europe political and economic stability returned with the Saxon-German Empire established by Otto I (936–973). In fact, the tenth century is actually the moment of 'the birth of the West'.[30] The European population climbed from about thirty-six million in 1000, to fifty-eight million in 1200 and seventy-nine million in 1300. Except for a sharp drop during the Black Death which hit Europe between 1347 and 1351, when about half the population died, numbers continued rising to about eighty-one million in 1500.

In China the Song (Sung) dynasty emerged in 960 ushering in a period of stability and cultural brilliance. The population jumped from sixty million in 1000 to 115 million in 1200. However, a sharp population decline occurred in the period between 1200 and 1400 with the overthrow of the Song in 1279 by the short-lived Yuan (Mongol) dynasty, leading to the emergence of the Ming in 1368. In 1331 the Black Death hit China with catastrophic effects with the population dropping to 75 million by 1400.

After the Black Death, there was a steady increase in world population to 1700 when numbers reached 610 million. This gradual increase continued despite the Little Ice Age with a temperature decrease of about 0.6°C (1.1° Fahrenheit) which lasted from after 1370 to about 1800; it probably occurred mainly in the northern hemisphere. By 1800 world population had reached 900 million and a billion around 1810–1820.

Population growth is exponential, meaning an increasing curve that grows more and more quickly as population increases in size. It starts slowly, but it has a way of ballooning after it has doubled several times. It took the entire history of the human race to reach one billion in the early-nineteenth century, but only another century to reach two billion. By 1960 we had reached three billion, by 1999 six billion and 7.9 billion by 2022.Though numbers are slowing, the UN estimates that world population is expected to reach 8.5 billion by 2030, 9.7 by 2050 and 10.9 by 2100.

Exponential growth after 1800 began in Britain with the industrial revolution, which was based on the country's extensive deposits of coal and iron ore, as well as a number of inventions like the spinning jenny and the steam engine. Of these, coal was most important because it was the energy source for industrialization. There was also an increasing movement to enclose and consolidate land-holdings by wealthy landowners in order to introduce industrialized agriculture. Peasant farmers were forced off their traditional small holdings that had been the basis of British agriculture for centuries and they crowded into industrial towns, providing workers for the factory system which was beginning to exploit the new machinery. This also paralleled the emergence of modern capitalism and the development of the banking system.

This all led to a complex of social issues that promoted population growth. In the early-nineteenth century overcrowding, poor housing, disease and infected water supplies in cities maintained a high death rate. But from the 1840s British working conditions improved; people married younger thus producing more children. Living standards increased and with a better diet and public health standards rising, people lived longer, leading to births outnumbering deaths. The threat of famine receded as improved transportation made it easier to move food around. Certainly, the famine of 1845–1849 caused the death of a million people in Ireland and forced many more to emigrate. But to a scandalous extent the famine was artificial because Ireland was still exporting cattle and large quantities of foodstuffs to England during the worst years of the 'great hunger'.

The Public Health Acts of 1848 and 1875 helped clean-up polluted British cities. Vaccination against smallpox became mandatory and later immunization of infants and children and the discovery and introduction in the 1920s of antibiotics increased survival rates for previously fatal diseases. Hospital hygiene improved, slums were cleared, sewerage and sanitation improved and a supply of potable water was connected to most dwellings.

For most of human history births only minimally outnumbered deaths, but from the early nineteenth century infant and child mortality rates dropped in Europe and North America as children survived into adulthood, so that nowadays worldwide births outnumber deaths about 2.5 to one. Increases in food production and distribution, regulations regarding the sanitary handling of food were introduced which led to higher standards of living and people living longer. Improvements in medical care, public health and sanitation, linked with much better medical knowledge and procedures, especially in the area of childbirth and child care also contributed to population increase.

The increasing use of fossil fuels was also important. Prior to the industrial revolution, useable energy depended on wind, water and the muscle power of animals and humans. But in the late-eighteenth century this constraint was broken by the steam engine. This opened-up an era of far looser constraints on energy supply and the global economy. Between 1800 and 2000 population grew more than six-fold, the global economy about fifty-fold, and energy forty-fold. Before the mid-twentieth century most population growth occurred in Europe and the Americas. This subsequently spread to the rest of the world. From about 1950 onwards a population explosion began in Asia, Latin America and Africa as advances in medicine and reproductive health, together with education and economic progress took hold.

While there have never been so many people, the actual dynamics of historical demography are still only partially understood, although reforms already detailed are obviously important causes. But the notion that these numbers can be endlessly sustained is pure fantasy, mostly nurtured by economists who simply don't comprehend limits. Equally fanciful are the projections of technophiles who assure us that somehow technology will provide resources, energy, food, and living space for ever-increasing numbers. What will happen if standards of living continue to improve toward developed world levels in countries like China? This is not to say that people in developing countries should not have a better life, but it is to say that Western standards of living are unsustainably high and cannot be reduplicated endlessly. The simple reality is that we are already far exceeding the earth's natural limits.

Theories of overpopulation

Serious discussion of overpopulation began with the Reverend Thomas Malthus (1766–1834), an Anglican clergyman and political economist, who published his *Essay on the Principle of Population as it affects the future improvement of society* in 1798, with a revised edition published in 1803. The *Essay* opposed the then popularly-held belief that high fertility and an increasing population added to the wealth and resources of a nation. Malthus argued that population increases geometrically, whereas food reserves grow arithmetically. By 'geometrically' he meant exponentially, that is a growth ratio that continually doubles from 2 to 4 to 8 to 16 to 32 and so on. He said that population increase 'goes on doubling itself every twenty-five years', thus putting great pressure on food supplies and resources which take time to plant, grow and produce. At the same time land was being swallowed-up by industrialization and urbanization, leading Malthus to call for limits to population growth. He enumerates the realities that shorten the natural duration of human life: 'Unwholesome occupations, severe labor and exposure to the seasons, extreme poverty, bad nursing of children, great towns, excesses of all kinds, the whole train of common diseases and epidemics, wars, plague, and famine.'[31] To limit family size, he called for moral restraint, late age of marriage, sexual abstinence and even celibacy for adults until they are economically able to support children. His book caused enormous controversy in its time and deeply influenced Charles Darwin.

Like many contemporary clergymen his theology was largely derived from Enlightenment thought and while his views developed to some extent over his lifetime, he believed that we came to know God only through a kind of natural theology by observing nature and its laws, rather than through biblical revelation and church doctrine. Given his pessimistic views on population, he was often accused of lacking faith in the generosity of God. Others said he ignored the biblical command to be 'fruitful and multiply' (Genesis 1:28), especially in terms of his call for the poor to practice moral restraint and keep their numbers down through late age of marriage. As a clergyman, he opposed contraception as immoral, primitive as it was in 1798. His views were pretty much ignored by the Anglican church of his time and contemporary evangelical and fundamentalist Christians have turned him into a kind of ogre. There has been on-going debate since Malthus' time about the accuracy of his claims.

Until the first part of the twentieth century contraception and birth control was seen as a moral issue. It was not until Marie Stopes (1880–1958) in Britain and Margaret Sanger (1879–1966) in the US that contraception came to be seen primarily as a medical issue. These two women were the pioneers of the reproductive health movement, planned parenthood, women's rights and birth control. But it was not until the 1960s that universal contraception became available with the introduction of the contraceptive pill.

Despite the optimism and economic growth of the decades between 1950 and 1970, the fact that world population almost doubled in that time led to concern about human numbers and the profligate use of resources. This concern came to a head when the Club of Rome published its 1972 report, *The Limits to Growth*. The report was based on the work of an international team of researchers at the Massachusetts Institute of Technology, who examined population, agricultural production, the use of non-renewable resources, industrial output, and pollution. They predicted that increasing human consumption and use of resources would lead to the earth reaching its supply limits within a century, if not before.

Similar views, but more focused on population, were expressed by Paul Ehrlich of Stanford University whose best-known books, *The Population Bomb* (1968) and *The Population Explosion* (co-authored with his wife Anne Ehrlich in 1990), were deliberately designed to provoke readers with a sense that we are living in a very dangerous period and heading for population catastrophe. Ehrlich and others argued that there must be a massive reduction in human numbers and a redistribution of material resources from the rich to the poor. They claimed that what was actually happening, especially in the US, was that money was taken from the poor and given to the rich through tax breaks. Ehrlich maintained that the optimum population of the earth was between 1.5 and two billion people and that we had to move towards 'population shrinkage' or depopulation. If population went to nine billion in 2050, Ehrlich expected starvation, disease, war, epidemics and worldwide plague, leading to a 'vast die-off'. He told *The Guardian* in 2012 that 'We have one billion hungry people now and we're going to add 2.5 billion', with 1.3 billion people living on less than US$1.25 a day.[32] Ehrlich argues that we must turn away from pro-natalist views which have dominated culture and religion for most of history, because in the past high infant mortality and an early average age of death meant that people often struggled just to replace themselves.

But the discussion of population lost much of its respectability from the mid-1980s onwards, following the forced sterilization policies of successive Congress Party governments in India in the 1970s, and the one-child policy in China which began in 1981 and which was lifted to a two-child policy in January 2016. While these policies were draconian, given the population pressures that both countries are still facing, they are understandable. The Chinese policy successfully cut the population increase from 5.81 children per woman in 1970 to 1.55 in 2013.[33]

Without doubt these programs have been cast in a very negative light by associating them with the eugenics movement, human rights violations and medical mismanagement. In India it was mainly the poor who were targeted for birth control programs like vasectomies. A critic of these programs is Matthew Connelly, whose 2008 book *Fatal Misconception* has been influential.[34] The book tells the story of how the World Bank, the United Nations and philanthropic organizations like the Ford and Rockefeller Foundations, as well as family planning groups and other wealthy 'do-gooders' made grievous mistakes by systematically devaluing women in poor countries by imposing contraception programs on them, sometimes without their consent and with no care or follow-up. Conolly correctly points out that in contrast to China and India, Thailand and Indonesia have been very successful in population control for many years. Essentially, his book is the case for the prosecution of arrogant family planners and population controllers, but it's unbalanced because it fails to acknowledge the good work that has been done and how difficult it is to confront an issue like overpopulation, especially in developing countries. While acknowledging the mistakes that Connelly points out, I argue that the situation we currently face means that human freedom is not an absolute value without limitation. It needs to be situated within the larger normative moral context of the priority of the natural world.

Most countries in the Western world have nowadays seen their populations fall to ZPG or below, with replacement coming from immigration. While we know that the greatest threat to the natural world comes from *both* the increase in the human population and the increasing demand for on-going resource exploitation to support growth, it still remains extremely difficult to make population a mainstream political issue. The result is that we are living in an era of massive extinctions and biodiversity loss. This is not the first time this has happened; we know that the earth has already experienced five mass extinction events. The most recent was some 65 million years ago in the Cretaceous period when the dinosaurs disappeared. This was probably caused by an increase in volcanic activity, possible asteroid impacts and climate change. Later in the book I will return to this contemporary extinction event.

What we do know is that this time humankind alone is the primary cause of mass extinction. As the International Union for the Conservation of Nature (ICUN) says bluntly, humankind is 'almost wholly responsible for the unprecedented extinction scenarios that are currently being played-out'.[35] We humans are now an out-of-control species who face the danger of making the only home we have completely uninhabitable. The consequences are clear: we will eventually join all the other species that we have been driven to extinction.

4

Population: A Truly Difficult Topic

Population denial

'Never say never' is a cliché, and sometimes it's wise advice. Whatever, I'm going to use the 'never' word in the next three sentences. In all human history we've never before been in a situation like the one we're in now. Never before have there been so many of us. Never before have we destroyed so much of the natural structures of the planet and threatened the survival of millions of other species whose lives enrich the marvellous diversity of earth.

What we're facing is unique for one simple reason: there are just too many of us. Our overwhelming numbers, our rate of increase and our standards of living are wiping out other species, destroying landscapes, polluting and asset-stripping the oceans, creating human-induced climate change and debasing the very life-systems of earth with the mining of coal, and the extraction of oil, gas and other pollutants. The result: our planet will not only become increasingly uninhabitable for other species, but also for us, our children and grandchildren. The simple fact is that we have become the most acute moral issue that we face.

This is a completely new challenge and we are particularly obtuse in facing it. We claim to be *sapiens*, wise and rational, yet many still refuse to accept realities like climate change that are staring us in the face. Why is this? What is it in our human make-up, psychology, economics and contemporary culture that makes it so difficult to confront the need for depopulation? Why are we in denial about it?

First, while many people generally recognize population overload, it doesn't really strike a chord with them. As humans we are specialists in compartmentalizing issues and 'short-termism'. As long as things are stable and comfortable now and our needs are being met, then seemingly down-the-track problems are put off; they only worry experts. Scientists often feel like they're talking to themselves when their rational, evidence-based arguments don't cut any ice with politicians and decision makers, let alone the general public. Perhaps the reason is that it's easy enough to present scientific and statistical evidence, but people often find that overwhelming, too complex, too much to take in. Unable to deal with it, many simply dismiss it from their minds. They feel impotent before such monumental, worldwide issues, which they see as being for the UN, or experts or decision-makers to solve. Sure, in many countries, politicians are taking scientific advice about COVID-19, but the pandemic is an immediate, pressing issue that can't be avoided. It is the long-term issues like escalating population that tend to be ignored, or put on the long finger.

We are also in denial because our economics are so short term. The capitalist market growth imperative makes it particularly difficult to deal with questions of the environment, biodiversity and overpopulation. Modern neo-liberal economics is actually based on a totally irrational principle: the notion that a finite world can produce an infinite source of raw materials that endlessly underpins unlimited, unending economic growth. Thus stated, it is, of course, nonsense, but that doesn't stop pro-growth apologists from assuming that if an economy is not constantly growing exponentially, then disaster is just around the corner. According to neo-liberals, for economic growth to occur you need workers to churn out products and consumers to purchase them, and the more consumers there are, the better. This, in turn, is posited on the notion that there is an infinite supply of raw materials from which these consumer items can be made. Anyone suggesting a reduction in the size of the population and thus in the number of workers and consumers, is uttering rank heresy and must be shouted down, and often is. The usual argument is that population decline undermines economic growth and weakens a developed country's strength and ability to support the bulge in the number of retired, aging people who are living longer.

Another reason why overpopulation is such a difficult topic to discuss in polite society is that it offends both the right and left wings of the political spectrum. For the right it suggests that you are anti-growth, want to reduce standards of living, or that you favor abortion, contraception, fertility control and sterilization, especially in developing countries. Many also assume that you want to limit the rights of couples to decide the number of children they wish to have. However, the most tedious, pharisaic moralisers are those on the left who accuse anyone discussing population limitation of racism, neo-colonialism, paternalism, or of dictating population size to developing countries. The result: politicians, with few exceptions, are unwilling to develop population policies. Even immigrant countries like the US, Canada and Australia have never developed or properly debated optimum carrying capacities. Only groups like the UK-based Population Matters, or Sustainable Population Australia have had the courage to try to keep these issues before the public, often at the risk of being called 'xenophobic' or worse, 'racist'.

You would expect something sensible on overpopulation from Green parties, but the fear of offending political correctness, particularly of the left, seems to have frightened them away from the issue. In an understandable attempt to appeal to a broad spectrum of voters, the Australian Greens, with ten representatives in the Australian parliament, usually take refuge in the rhetoric of 'a globally sustainable population', arguing that environmental impacts result from 'a range of factors including per capita consumption patterns and levels, distribution of resources, agricultural practices for domestic consumption and export, levels and types of industrial activity and production, urban design and transport options.' Certainly, they admit that the 'continuing rapid increase in the human population is drastically affecting national and international outcomes in environmental sustainability, human health and welfare, and other areas'.[36] But in the end, there is a failure to say clearly that the world is already overpopulated and that the sheer weight of numbers is having a horrendous impact on the environment.

The Canadian Greens at least place the population problem in an historical context and point out that with 7.9 billion people on the planet we're already running out of water. The New Zealand Greens, with ten members in Parliament, do focus on population. They say that 'New Zealand's population should not exceed the ecological carrying capacity of the country' and that parents should make 'informed decisions about family size and spacing'. They call for research on 'an optimum population level' and for New Zealand to 'accept our share of climate change refugees particularly from Pacific Island countries', as well as working 'cooperatively with other countries to address problems of overpopulation and environmentally unsustainable lifestyles'. With the exception of New Zealand, Green parties, which are supposedly dedicated to the environment, are unwilling to confront the issue of population head-on, so what hope can we have for mainstream politicians?

In their book *The Population Explosion* Anne and Paul Ehrlich ask: 'Why isn't everyone as scared as we are?' of overpopulation. They acknowledge that most people, including scientists, 'seldom make the connection between [environmental destruction] and the population problem, and thus remain unworried' about the increase in human numbers. They also refer to a 'colossal failure of education' for public indifference about population and comment that the media hardly ever connect ecological problems, global warming and extinction scenarios to population growth. But they then descend to caricature attacking the Catholic Church with its so-called 'social taboos'.[37] Sure, Catholicism must take some blame because of papal ideology opposing contraception, but sheeting home all blame to the church is nonsense. It's as though neo-liberal economics with its ever-expanding need for gormless consumers of useless products, post-modern individualism, gross over-consumption, political short-termism, widespread corruption, instability in developing countries and failures to provide reproductive health services for women, played no part. But the question posed by Anne and Paul Ehrlich remains: why aren't people scared? Well actually, there is one issue where a message connected to overpopulation is actually getting through—global warming.

Global warming

Overpopulation and global warming are linked and the nexus between them will become acute by the late-2020s. Across the world there is increasing drought, water shortages and rivers drying-up. Sea-level rises and coastal flooding, especially in the fertile deltas of the Ganges-Brahmaputra rivers in Bangladesh and India, where more than 120 million people live, will lead to enormous numbers of climate refugees, as people try to escape their increasingly unliveable homelands. We are also seeing once-in-a-thousand-year storms and hurricanes, like those in Florida and Louisiana in late-August 2005 and in the southern US and Central America in August–September 2017, which together cost $250 billion in damage. Increasingly the Philippines is being hit by extreme category five typhoons with winds up to 265km/h (164mp/h) and thousands of people effected or killed.

Other issues linked to global warming are intolerable heat waves, widespread wildfires, like those in Australia in December–January 2002–2003, January 2009 and September to January 2019–2020 (when three billion native animals were killed), and the US West Coast in mid-November 2018 and August–September 2020. There were also lethal heatwaves in Europe in 1999 and again in August 2003 when 70,000 people died, widespread wildfires in the summer of 2018 and 2019 in Spain and Germany and temperatures in August–September 2018 that reached levels in Europe that were the highest since records began in 1880. The North American West coast experienced the highest temperatures on record in July 2021 together with extensive wildfires with the temperature in Death Valley, California reaching 133F (56C). There have also been widespread fires in Brazil's Amazon region, most of them deliberately lit.

The impact of global warming was highlighted when in mid-2019 there were even wildfires across the Arctic Circle, including in Alaska, as the planet experienced the hottest June on record. According to the World Meteorological Organization, such conflagrations have not been experienced in the last 10,000 years. The thick clouds of smoke resulting from these fires can be seen from space. On 9 June 2020 the temperature in the Arctic reached an astonishing 30°C. The widespread danger here is that the permafrost will melt, releasing methane gas which is far more potent than carbon dioxide as a heat-trapping gas.[38] At present methane comprises some 25% of global warming gases, but there is a serious danger that if the methane trapped in the Arctic permafrost is released, the result could be catastrophic.

Clearly climate change is impacting with the world already 1°C warming above pre-industrial levels. For instance, the Australian climate has warmed 1.44°C since measuring began in 1910.[39] The

Paris climate agreement of 2015 set a limit of 2°C warming, but that is completely inadequate. The aim now is to try to halt warming at less than 1.5°C, but that is certainly no Nirvana. 1.5°C would still have catastrophic effects, including intense storms, searing heat waves, wildfires, water shortages, droughts, mass extinctions and 90% of coral reefs gone, including Australia's Great Barrier Reef. To prevent us reaching 1.5°C we will have to cut greenhouse emissions by 45% by 2030 compared to what they were in 2010. By 2050 we would have to reduce all emissions to zero. The likelihood of us reaching those goals is becoming more difficult, due largely to the lack of political will in many countries and the influence of vested interests, such as fossil fuel lobby and its media minions.

If we don't take global warming seriously, the results will be catastrophic in many countries. In their illustrated guide to the findings of the IPCC, *Dire Predictions*, Lee Kump and Michael Mann describe how drought, heat, sea-level rise and overpopulation will quickly lead to chaos in countries like Nigeria: 'Increasingly severe drought in West Africa will generate a mass migration from the highly populous interior of Nigeria to its coastal mega-city, Lagos. Already threatened by rising sea levels, Lagos will be unable to accommodate this massive influx of people. Squabbling over dwindling oil reserves in the Niger river delta, combined with potential for state corruption, will add to the factors contributing to massive social unrest.'[40] The reality is that many regions of the world are going to be under similar stress by 2050 or earlier. People without hope, especially if they are environmental refugees, tend to get angry. If there are enough of them, they will constitute a real challenge to major institutions and nation states. A place where global warming and overpopulation is already impacting people is in the low-lying Pacific country of Kiribati. Here we can see what the future holds for all of us.

An overpopulated paradise

The republic of Kiribati (pronounced 'Key-ri-bas') is one of the most isolated places on earth, but it has a serious overpopulation problem. This is compounded by the fact that the landscape itself is drowning, the direct result of global warming. In fact, no matter where you look on South Tarawa Atoll the ocean is flooding in everywhere. Tidal surges break down the sea walls that people endlessly rebuild and 'the water comes in and takes away everything, even our houses', Tearei Tekita, a local woman says. Kiribati will be largely uninhabitable in twenty years, its population becoming the world's first national group of climate refugees.

South Tarawa, on tiny Tarawa Atoll, is the Republic's capital. It's literally in the centre of the Pacific Ocean, just 1.45° north of the Equator and 7° west of the International Date Line. Every morning it's the first place in the world to see the dawn. South Tarawa is densely populated. Here some 70,000 people, more than half of the country's population, are crammed onto a narrow strip of land with a total area of just 15.76 square kilometres (6.8 square miles). That is just over 4000 people per square kilometre (approximately 9,400 per square mile), a population density greater than Los Angeles. Spread over thirty-three islands, the total land surface of Kiribati is just 811 square kilometres (313 square miles). Most of Kiribati is the Pacific Ocean and its total area is equivalent in size to the continental United States.

In 1950 Kiribati's population was 33,000, in 1974 53,800. The total population of Kiribati in mid-2021 was estimated at 121,390.[41] Current population growth is 2.2% and the 2020 fertility rate is 3.58 children per woman. If this rate continues Kiribati's population by 2050 could be 200,000, although the reality is that the country will be uninhabitable long before then. Infant and child mortality is high, as is youth unemployment.

The reason for South Tarawa's high population density is both the high birth rate and the crowding-in of people from the outer islands because of coastal flooding due to global warming and a lack of medical and other services. What limited employment there is in the country is largely in South Tarawa and population density places enormous pressure on the services available. There are many health problems: dengue fever, typhoid, cholera, diarrhoea and other mosquito borne diseases are widespread, especially in South Tarawa. Poor sanitation and a lack of good nutrition, as well as eating semi-raw seafood and bacterial contamination from human waste can lead to food poisoning. The country's economy is unsustainable with what little income there is coming from its marine resources, fishing licenses and seafood exports which have provided a revenue stream. However, with just one patrol boat, covering the country's enormous expanse of ocean, it is almost impossible to police international fishing. Most food, fresh fruit and vegetables have to be imported. Kiribati is still one of the least developed countries in the Pacific region and is still very dependent on overseas aid. Australia is Kiribati's major donor with a grant of A$27.3 million in 2020, with the other major donors being the World Bank, the Asian Development Bank, New Zealand and Japan. The Chinese are also becoming increasingly influential on the present government.

Linked to overpopulation is the threat from climate change and rising ocean levels. The highest point on Tarawa atoll is just three meters (9.8 feet) above sea level. With rising ocean levels there is a long-term threat of complete submersion. But the atolls will become uninhabitable before that. Fresh water supplies are already compromised by sea water leaching into ground water, so that people are dependent on harvesting rainwater. Salt water is already polluting the few crops there are. There is also an increasing threat of storm surges and king tides. A storm surge hit Tarawa in March 2015, flooding and damaging many buildings, including the hospital. While flooding makes life on South Tarawa even more difficult, on the outer islands many coastal villages have been simply washed-away.

With the exception of the raised coral island of Banaba (or Ocean Island), the land surface of Kiribati is made up of low coral atolls. Coral is a living organism dependent on a delicately balanced ocean temperature. Even small rises in temperature result in coral bleaching and eventual death. This is already happening. Another danger is that a shift in weather patterns could place Kiribati in the Pacific hurricane belt. All of this places it at risk of being one of the first countries in the world to become uninhabitable through global warming. Still the world ignores the disaster facing the *I-Kiribati*, the people of Kiribati. As former President Anote Tong says: 'Even the polar bears are being considered, but not the people being effected' by climate change. Tong developed a much-criticized plan to resettle the entire population elsewhere, probably Fiji. This raises the unprecedented question as to whether a country can continue to exist when its territory has literally disappeared? Perhaps something of the culture and language could be preserved if the people moved to Fiji, New Zealand or Australia, but what would happen to the country's sovereignty? These questions remain unanswered.

President Tong, who left office in 2016, tried to raise public consciousness of the threat of overpopulation, particularly in Tarawa. His government attempted to encourage people to return to the other islands, but few left because of the lack of services and a subsistence level life-style outside the capital. The government also attempted to introduce a family planning program, but it hasn't been particularly successful because of the cultural and family tradition of Pacific people of having many children. Contraception rates in Oceania are well below UN global averages. People in Tarawa are simply not interested in, or are ignorant of contraception and family planning education is often culturally inappropriate. While to an extent supported by the Protestant churches, family planning was opposed by the recently-retired Catholic bishop, Paul Mea. Like the rest of the Pacific, Kiribati is a strongly Christian country, with about 56% of the people Catholic and 35% Protestant. The strong cultural tradition of big families is encouraged by the churches.

What the future holds for Kiribati remains to be seen. Under President Tong, the country was very active in international climate change discussions, but not everyone agreed with his assessment of the country's future. Scientists have pointed out that coral atolls are dynamic structures that can grow with sea-level rise, and in 2016 a new government was elected with more inward-looking policies, focusing on increasing revenue to promote employment and education, reducing poverty and persuading people to return to the outer islands. Current President Taneti Maamau doesn't believe that Kiribati will go under and he believes that God will save 'our beautiful lands'.

In many ways this reflects the current opinion of most *I-Kiribati*. Very few people are making plans to leave and the majority are hopeful, if apprehensive, about the future. Many see global warming as a long-term problem. 'We don't want to think about it,' they say. Lulu de Boer, an American journalist with *I-Kiribati* ancestors says that 'people here don't … know much about climate change. If you try to explain to someone who has lived his entire life here that giant icebergs are melting, it's not something that they can really picture … There are

40

no icebergs here and it's hard to imagine the magnitude of an iceberg when you are on a island that is so small.' Even young people, who will be most impacted by global warming, are sceptical. One sixteen-year-old boy in a Catholic high school says: 'God has created things for a reason. They say that the rising sea levels happen when the icebergs melt in the north and south pole. But in the bible they say that God created the sun to evaporate that. So I don't believe the sea is really rising. There's an old saying in the bible by Noah about the flooding of the sea. According to that, it would never happen again. So I believe in that.'[42] These views are re-enforced by religious leaders. Many trust God's promise to Noah that there will be no more floods. One young girl is very honest: 'The reason why I am still believing [in the bible] … is because I'm afraid. And I don't know how to get all my fifty or sixty family members away from here. That's why I'm afraid, but I'm putting it behind me. Because I just don't know what to do.'[43]

This semi-denialist position is understandable given that climate change is totally outside the *I-Kiribati*'s control. In the end, it comes down to who you trust? To the people of Kiribati God seems a much better bet than coal exporting countries like Australia that have done virtually nothing to limit their own output of carbon dioxide producing the climate change that is drowning the islands. In the end, Anote Tong will be proved right. The problem is that with a 1.5°C rise in temperature, the long-term prognosis for Kiribati and its neighbour Tuvalu, or the Maldives in the northern Indian Ocean, is disaster. Given that we are already struggling to hold climate change to a 1.5°C increase and there has been a tripling of the melt rate of the Antarctic ice sheet in the last five years and the Greenland ice sheet is also in melt-down, the future for the *I-Kiribati* looks bleak indeed.

Kiribati is a foretaste of what is yet to come for much of the rest of the world. As Anote Tong says, 'What the world has got to understand is that we would be the first people who would be dislocated as a result of climate change. But I can guarantee you, we won't be the last … People have got to understand that its going to happen and its going to be on a massive scale', with whole populations dislocated. Kiribati is a study in miniature of what will happen right across the world.

The contrast between the situation in Kiribati and West Africa's

Niger is stark. Even though sea level rise will soon make Kiribati uninhabitable, the number of people we are dealing with – about 120,000 – is manageable. Australia, for example, took 160,323 migrants in 2018–2019, mainly from countries utterly remote to Australia. As leading Pacific nations, Australia and New Zealand have an absolute responsibility for their Pacific neighbours and when the worst-case scenario is realized in Kiribati, these two countries have an unequivocal moral responsibility to help the *I-Kiribati*. Niger has nothing like that going for it, because its neighbours are already over-populated, borders are closed due to COVID-19, so there is nowhere for its people to go.

Refugees and immigrants

Discussion of population has become even more fraught over the last decade due to the large-scale movement of people across the world – temporarily halted by COVID-19 – escaping danger and persecution from war and religious strife in the Middle East and poverty, violence and overpopulation in Africa, Central America and parts of Asia. The problem for discussion of overpopulation is that often in the public mind the question becomes conflated with issues concerning immigration and refugees. This makes it even more difficult to discuss human numbers rationally.

Here a distinction needs to be made between refugees and immigrants. 'Refugee' is one of those words that people use without precising its meaning. According to the 1951 UNHCR Refugee Convention, a refugee is 'someone who has fled their country and is unwilling to return … owing to a well-founded fear of being persecuted for reasons of race, religion, nationality, membership of a particular social group, or political opinion.' This definition, which some see as too narrow, dates from the period after the Second World War when people were very conscious of the Holocaust, as well as massacres of other races and groups like gypsies. Various other broader definitions of the word refugee have been proposed, such as the the Cartagena Declaration of 1984, which talks about 'persons who have fled their country because their lives, safety or freedom have been threatened by generalized violence, foreign aggression, internal conflicts, massive violation of human rights or other circumstances which have seriously disturbed public order'.

Refugees are protected by the international legal principle of non-refoulement (from the French *refouler* meaning to 'drive back'), which the 1951 Refugee Convention defines as a guarantee that 'no contracting state shall expel or return a refugee in any manner whatsoever to the frontiers of territories where his life or freedom would be threatened on account of his race, religion, nationality, membership of a particular social group or political opinion'. Worldwide, at the end of 2020 there were 26.4 million refugees, around half of whom are under the age of 18.[44] The term 'asylum seeker' is often used interchangeably with the word refugee, but strictly-speaking asylum seeker refers to a person seeking refugee status, but who has not yet received it. In international law refugees and asylum seekers have a right to protection and support, no matter how they arrived in a country of refuge.

Of course, not all those arriving in developed countries are strictly-speaking refugees. Many are escaping economic, environmental and overpopulation problems at home and sometimes it's difficult to distinguish them from refugees. Many have undertaken dangerous journeys to reach a developed country. For example, those from sub-Saharan Africa will have usually crossed the Sahara Desert, with its risks of dehydration, starvation, armed tribes, Libyan thugs and a Mediterranean crossing, to reach southern Europe. Some die on the journey, and those who make it to north Africa often get bogged-down in conflict-torn Libya. Since 2019 an increasing number are coming through Morocco and heading for Spain. No matter which way they come, their aim is to move through Italy, Greece and Spain to get to Germany, the UK or Scandinavia. With COVID-19 and very tight border controls, many of these people are cooped-up in refugee camps on islands like Greece's Lesbos.

Across the Atlantic people from Central America are trying to get to the US and Canada. Many of them come from Honduras, Guatemala, El Salvador, Cuba and Venezuela. With much of northern and central Mexico controlled by drug cartels, many have to travel through gang-dominated regions to reach the southern border of the US. They are often escaping unemployment, violence, gang warfare, corruption, overpopulation, dire poverty and political instability in their own countries. As long as the root causes remain, the flow of people will continue. But they face a deeply polarized US, particularly under the anti-immigrant policies of Donald Trump. At least President Joe Biden promises a more humane, compassionate policy toward asylum seekers.

World-wide the issue of people seeking a better life has become increasingly fraught and divisive, particularly in Europe and the US. Smaller countries like Austria and Hungary, or even Poland, where people feel their culture is under threat from immigrant influxes, have elected populist, anti-immigrant governments.

But what we are facing now is just a foretaste of the tsunami of people, be they refugees or immigrants, that is to come. I've already mentioned the 100,000 square kilometre (38,600 square miles) low-lying Ganges-Brahmaputra delta in Bangladesh and West Bengal. Most of this coastal zone is less than five meters (sixteen feet) above sea level and much of it is subsiding with groundwater already being polluted by seawater. This process is exacerbated by global warming. The region already has an annual tropical rainfall of sixty to eighty inches per year, which causes widespread flooding and this rainfall is expected to increase. The water-flow in the Ganges-Brahmaputra is increasingly boosted by melting glaciers in the Himalayas, also caused by global warming. With their living space drowned, where will these 120 million environmental refugees go? Among the biodiversity that could be lost in the Delta is the world heritage listed Sundarbans mangrove forest, probably the largest mangrove forest (140,000 hectares or 540.5 square miles) in the world. It is home to many species of birds, the Bengal tiger and other threatened species.

'Death spiral demographics' and over-consumption

Despite these threatening scenarios, those advocating serious discussion of population are often dismissed by those who claim that overpopulation has already been thoroughly debunked, and that in fact we're experiencing the opposite, so-called 'death spiral demographics', as the business magazine *Forbes* calls it. *Forbes* points to plunging birth rates and longer life expectancy in developed countries like Italy, Poland and Spain, significantly all predominately

Catholic countries.[45] Economists seem particularly obsessed with low birth rates leading to economic slow-downs, which in the neo-liberal worldview is heresy.

David Attenborough is someone who has not allowed the threat of 'death spiral demographics', or the politically correct silence him. Through his TV documentaries he has done much to make living, sentient creatures real for us, thus deepening our concern for the protection of the natural world. He has often referred to the 'absurd taboo' of *not* speaking about population pressures, given that the greatest threat to the natural world and other species is humankind. He says bluntly that there 'seems to be some bizarre taboo around the subject'.[46] 'We are a plague on the earth,' he says. 'It's coming home to roost. It's not just climate change, it's sheer space, places to grow food for this enormous horde. Either we limit our population growth, or the natural world will do it for us.'[47] To drive the point home, Attenborough says: 'We can't go on increasing at the rate human beings are increasing forever, because Earth is finite and you can't put infinity into something that is finite … So if we don't do something about it then the world will do something about it … [and] we will starve.' The one hope he has is that 'wherever women are given political control of their bodies, where they have the vote, education, appropriate medical facilities and they can read and have rights … the birth rate falls, there's no exceptions to that.'[48]

Attenborough notwithstanding, there are still enormously powerful vested interests in government, business and media who want to stifle this discussion. Their aim is to maintain inflated rates of growth, especially in western countries which have already reached ZPG, through high rates of immigration. Business lobbies are often facilitated by a kind of wilful self-censoring by journalists, educationalists and politicians who seem to perceive discussion of overpopulation as taboo. Even the environmentally-aware Pope Francis underestimates the importance of the problem. In his otherwise admirable encyclical on the environment, *Laudato si'* (2015), he dismisses population growth and is critical of 'reproductive health' which he sees as a Western plot to control poorer countries.

Sure, inertia still infects many people when confronted with overpopulation, but the good thing is that when the public wake-up and sort out fact from fiction, as they are beginning to on climate change, public opinion shifts and people move ahead of governments. Interestingly many large corporations have also embraced the reality of human induced climate change and are attempting to deal with it. With the election of the Biden administration in Washington, we will see the US return to doing something about global warming. Certainly, as social justice advocates maintain, rates of consumption also have to be considered when talking about sustainability and the impact on a given environment is actually population *times* consumption, that is population multiplied by the rate of consumption. In this equation people from the poorest countries per capita consume the least resources, but it is also true that their high fertility exacerbates the problem.

In the developed West it is over-consumption of often unnecessary products that chews-up non-renewable resources and creates enormous piles of trash, much of it non-biodegradable. For instance, Australia has been one of the most wasteful countries in the world with its citizenry using ten million plastic bags per day, 85% of which ended-up in landfill. However, in September 2018 the major supermarket chains ceased giving out free plastic bags for purchases and anyone wanting a reusable bag had to pay for it. Within three months some 1.5 billion bags were saved from entering landfill, an 80% drop. The UK achieved a similar result. However, the average Australian family still throws out about $3500 worth of food; that's about one ton every year. One third of household trash is food waste which rots in landfill producing methane.[49]

All of these issues are interconnected and can't be solved one at a time, which is the way we tend to operate because that seemingly makes problems more manageable. The real challenge is facing the whole picture. 'Overpopulation [is] worsened by overconsumption … and the use of environmentally malign technologies, all … exacerbated by socio-political and economic inequality.'[50] Because all these issues are inter-connected, we can't delink a decrease in consumption from overpopulation. Both have to be dealt with together.

Linked to this nexus of consumption and population growth is the fact that we also face the reality of a fast-emerging middle class in China where patterns of consumption are sharply increasing. *Business*

Insider, reporting research by McKinsey, claims that '76% of China's urban population will be considered middle class by 2022'. That is, by 2022 about 550 million Chinese will have roughly comparable consumption rates to the West.[51] Whether this level of economic growth can be maintained remains to be seen, but economists are eternal optimists. Whatever, we need to recognize that enormous resources will be needed and the consequences for the natural world will be disastrous. The situation in India is sometimes seen as comparable to China, but that is now questioned. Before 2015 there was much talk of an emerging Indian middle class that would provide a vast market for Western goods and luxuries. But the simple reality is that India still has an enormous disparity between rich and poor, which to some extent China has bridged. If there is a middle class in India, people in it are still on very low incomes by developed world standards. The reality is that India still has a vast underclass of about 840 million who live on less than $5 a day.[52]

Given all these complex realities, what we going to do?

5

What are Our Options?

Technology is the solution?

Like it or not, by 2050, unless something radical is done, or nuclear war, or a catastrophic pandemic that is very much worse than COVID-19 intervenes, there will be 9.74 billion people on earth. By any rational standard, let alone by any standard of protecting the environment and preserving biodiversity, that's far too many people. Nevertheless, there are still those who think we can manage very well, and there are even some who think the bigger the population, the better.

When they first propounded their views in the 1960s and 1970s, thinkers like Paul Ehrlich, who were usually biologists, were widely criticized, especially by economists and technologists, who argued that the earth could support much larger populations leading to an increase in economic prosperity. The idea was that population growth would level out without interference from us as standards of living rose and education became universal. While most concede that the world is very crowded and there is enormous pressure on resources and biodiversity, economists tend to be optimists about the future and see each additional human as adding a unit of production and consumption. Biologists tend to be pessimists and see every new baby as another mouth to feed using up space and resources.

Most technophiles support the optimistic view. They claim new technologies will allow us to cope not only with the present population, but even with larger numbers in the future. The argument is that the more people there are, the more brains there will be working on earth's problems, the more ingenuity to develop technical solutions and more wealth to deal with those problems. One of the technological solutions already being used is genetic modification (GM) of plants. This is when the constituent genetic characteristics of a living organism are deliberately manipulated through biotechnology to create strains that are more productive and more resistant to disease and drought. GM plants have been around for several decades and many of us have been consuming genetically modified soybeans, canola and corn during that time. The arguments for genetic modification are that these plants can be used to feed the hungry, that the use of pesticides can be reduced, that less water is used, that they can be packed with nutrients to enhance the value of the food and that they are resistant to drought.

But not everybody agrees that GM is morally justifiable. The Irish environmentalist-priest, Sean McDonagh, says that patenting of organisms 'is a fundamental attack on the understanding of life as interconnected, mutually dependent and a gift of God to be shared with everyone. Patenting opts for an atomized, isolated understanding of life', divorcing the manipulated plants from the bigger reality of life in the natural world.[53] At its core genetic engineering is an expression of human arrogance, an assumption that nature is subject to our manipulation, a contempt for natural processes. McDonagh and others are also concerned about increasingly private, corporate control of the world's food supplies and food research. They point out that multinational corporations often use patenting laws 'to impose control, robbing poorer nations of their genetic riches and rights over the seeds they have bred'. To maintain control over their patents these companies introduce a 'terminator gene' to make the plants sterile. At first many saw GM as a solution to hunger and under-nourishment. However, there has been a reaction against it because it 'hands over control of the staple foods of the world into the hands of a few wealthy corporations'.[54] Also, there is increasing scepticism about the increase in yields that many claim and that just as much water is used as with ordinary crops.

Another technological proposal, this time to solve global warming, is geoengineering. This involves direct intervention in atmospheric and earth systems to deal with climate change. Geoengineers propose two ways of removing CO2 gasses from the atmosphere. One is solar radiation management (SRM) and the other is carbon dioxide removal (CDR). Essentially SRM, which is sometimes called stratospheric aerosol injection, aims to reflect the sun's heat rays away from the earth and back into space to reverse global warming. Geoengineers propose that reflective aerosols be spread in the high atmosphere, mimicking what happens when a major volcano erupts and spreads similar particles which reflect the sun's rays. SRM is a radical human manipulation of atmospheric processes and in an integrated biosphere no one has the slightest idea of the long-term consequences of SRM.

The most basic CDR proposal is to plant many more trees, on one estimate a billion or more, taking up a space of about the size of Canada. This solution appeals because it is natural, but it will take time. Another CDR proposal is to increase the phytoplankton in the ocean. These are tiny organisms that absorb sun light, CO_2 and water to produce most of the world's oxygen through photosynthesis. When phytoplankton die, they sink into the deep ocean taking the ingested carbon with them. The CDR proposal is to add iron particles to the ocean to promote the growth of phytoplankton. 'The idea is to take advantage of minerals synthesised by iron-oxidising bacteria that feed on the tiny spark of energy they generate by transferring electrons between iron and oxygen. This process produces rust minerals as by-products, which are of the right chemical composition to be used by the phytoplankton that help remove carbon dioxide from the atmosphere.'[55] Again, we're dealing with a major intervention into natural processes with completely unknown long-term effects.

Many think that any form of genetic modification poses a threat to natural biodiversity. Geoengineering is even more dangerously radical because, it is a deliberate and untested human intervention to counter natural systems that have evolved over millennia. It may be unconscious, but it is extraordinarily arrogant, because it assumes that some engineer knows more about nature than nature itself. It also reflects the naïve anthropocentric arrogance of abstract specialists living in ivory towers. The basic problem is that many economists and technophiles tend to be crudely utilitarian in their approach, seemingly lacking any moral compass or ethical principles. The theory is: if it works, it's OK. This approach is quite dominant and pervasive in our culture and many uncritically see technology as a universal panacea for all the problems we face. It certainly has a role to play, but it is not a magic solution. One of the profound intellectual and practical fissures running through the contemporary world is between those who believe that technology is a form of salvation and those who hold to the much more traditional faith of trust in the rhythms of the natural world and the bio-systems that have been evolved by nature. Those who trust nature are not Luddites who reject technology, but they see it in perspective as an ancillary tool. In the final chapter I will return to the blandishments of technology as a form of deliverance.

The effects of overpopulation

Whatever about technology as salvation, the reality is that in many countries, overpopulation is having disastrous effects. As former US Vice-President Al Gore says: 'Societies that learned over the course of hundreds of centuries to eke out a living within fragile ecosystems are suddenly confronted in a single generation with the necessity of feeding, clothing and sheltering two or three times as many individuals within those same ecosystems.'[56] These countries can no longer afford to care for their fragile environments and feel pressured to focus solely on human needs. In Niger, for example, unstoppable human demands put enormous pressure on ecosystems, with resultant droughts, famines and expanding desert in a country that is already largely desert. While overall world fertility rates are dropping, this is not true of the poorest countries, particularly in sub-Saharan Africa and in the region stretching from Afghanistan and Pakistan to across northern India. These regions that will drive world population growth until 2100.

However, there is some good news. Between the years 1950 and 2017 there was a global decline in fertility rates as women had less children, although the decline is not consistent across all countries. To get some perspective: worldwide in 1950 women had, on average, 4.7 children in their lifetimes. By 2017 that rate had halved to 2.4 per woman. That said, research reveals huge differences between countries. Women in West Africa are still having 6.3 children per woman, whereas women on the island of Cyprus are having only one child per woman. Economically developed countries in Europe, North America, Australia, South Korea, Japan, Thailand and Taiwan have low fertility rates, with population increase coming through immigration.

A hopeful note in terms of population reduction is China.

According to a China Academy of Social Studies 2018–2019 report on population, China's one child policy succeeded in cutting the population to such an extent that there is now concern in the Chinese Communist Party about falling birth rates, so the Beijing government replaced the one-child policy with a two-child policy in 2015. The perceived problem is that the country's population will peak at 1.44 billion in 2029 and then decline to 1.36 billion by the middle of the century, dropping to 1.17 billion by 2065. Despite the turn-around in official Chinese government policy, many couples are still having only one child. With increasing educational standards and income levels, couples are putting-off marriage until they are in their thirties, thus delaying childbirth.

The fear of decreasing numbers usually leads those addicted to never-ending economic growth to panic because, as they see it, there are fewer workers to produce products and consumers to buy them. Pro-growth apologists often argue that there won't be enough able-bodied, working people paying tax to support a bulging group of aging, 'non-productive' people. Seemingly, no account is taken of the wisdom, experience and maturity of these older people. This specious argument ignores the fact that this is a short-term problem because as population numbers decrease the temporary bulge in retirees and older people will even out, allowing a new equilibrium to be attained as the smaller numbers stabilize.[57]

Even COVID-19 has been harnessed by pro-growth apologists. Australian demographer, Liz Allen, says she is fearful that the pandemic will lead to a reduction in the birth rate, that in turn will reduce the number of taxpayers needed to support an aging population. She talks about 'missing children' by which she means those who will never be born because COVID-19 will frighten people into postponing, or not having children. 'These are children that we will never see,' she says, 'and will never return to our demographic profile in a later time', essentially as consumers and taxpayers.[58] Underlying her argument is the fear that economic growth will be slowed down or even cease because the whole neo-liberal dogma is posited on the assumption of eternal economic growth. Pro-growth apologists are panicking in developed countries with high immigration intakes because of closed borders due to COVID-19. This could well lead to a re-assessment of immigration numbers in light of the carrying capacity of intake countries like Australia, Canada and the United States. The reality is we should rejoice that a lot of countries are reaching, have reached, or have fallen below the replacement rate of 2.1 children per women, because it means we are getting some basic control over numbers.

Depopulation

It is not just a question of reaching ZPG. The real challenge we face is depopulation, because the world is *already* over-populated and our enormous impact on the environment is causing disastrous consequences now. The steeper the fall in population numbers, the more hope there is for threatened species, biodiversity and posterity. We can't rest on our laurels at ZPG. We have a much harder road to hoe, especially in countries like Niger, Chad, Somalia, South Sudan and Afghanistan. These are the real challenges. Even though we know that the world population growth rate is slowly decreasing and that total numbers are growing at a slower rate than in the past sixty years, the absolute number of people in the world is still increasing at about 200,000 every day, or six million per month, or over seventy million a year. At that rate we reproduce the population of Australia every four months.

Exacerbating this situation is another key issue: the youth bulge. This refers to the fact that in many developing countries there is a very large population of people aged eighteen or younger who have just entered their fertile years and who can be expected to have three to four children per woman. This is particularly true of the least developed countries, especially those that have recently experienced, or are experiencing the trauma of war, genocide, or terrorism.

An example of this is Timor-Leste whose total land mass is 15,010 square kilometres, which is five times *less* than the total area of Scotland. The country experienced a violent separation from Indonesia in 2002. Its population in 1987 was 667,000. This had risen to 1.34 million in mid-2021, with a media age of 19.8 and a fertility rate of 4.34. The bulge is the result of recent improvements in nutrition and health services and a decline in infant mortality, as well as a response to the deaths of so many people during the Indonesian occupation. There is also an enormous bulge of young people in Africa, the Middle East and

South America of child-bearing age who will also have a longer life expectancy. An example is Sub-Saharan Africa where about 40% of the population is under 15, and nearly 70% under 30. This youth bulge can lead to social unrest, especially where there are large cohorts of young males with post-primary education. Disruption and violence can occur because these young men have expectations that are not being met, especially when they can't get employment. This form of internecine strife can be particularly vicious, as the 1991–2002 civil war in Sierra Leone showed, and there are many other examples across the world.

Given the youth bulge and the parlous economic and environmental situation in most African countries, there is already a massive exodus of people seeking better lives mainly in Europe, briefly stopped by border closures due to COVID-19. The majority of these emigrants are young men from Nigeria, Mali, Senegal, Ghana, Ivory Coast, Togo, Niger, Gambia, as well as Ethiopia and Eritrea. The problem in these source countries is tribal and civil conflict, poverty, high unemployment, corruption and political instability, all exacerbated by out-of-control population growth resulting in sometimes catastrophic environmental degradation. Overpopulation puts enormous pressure on communities, as people struggle just to get hold of life's basic necessities. Often young men are selected by their villages and communities to go to Europe get employment and send remittances back. If they are unsuccessful, their villages will often reject them if they try to return. Others, without any other option, risk their lives to escape in the hope of prosperity and stability in the West.

Overpopulation also puts pressure on food supplies, resulting in hunger being a reality for almost a billion people in the developing world. Global warming results in severe droughts, leading to famines, locust infestations and other natural disasters in Africa and elsewhere and these could become more common and geographically widespread making people increasingly dependent on imported food. According to the World Economic Forum's Global Risks Report (2018) there is a definite possibility that extreme weather events will create failures of staple crops like maize and wheat even in major exporting countries like the US, Canada and Australia. These countries are already experiencing major changes in weather patterns, resulting in widespread and more frequent droughts and crop failures. The simple reality is that the supply of food is not keeping up with demand. This has led to a large increase in the price of basic staples.

Then, to complicate things, there is COVID-19. Over-populated, developing countries like India, their health systems already weakened by HIV, tuberculosis, malaria and mosquito borne diseases, added to food shortages, malnutrition, droughts, locust infestation and other natural disasters, are now having to close down what work was available due to social distancing and the fear of infection. What has happened with COVID-19 is that social distancing is often impossible for poor people in over-crowded slums and favellas without reliable water supplies, let alone soap. In a country like India with a population of almost 1.4 billion, 20% of whom live below the poverty line, tight lock-downs and restrictions on movement mean that many poor people have lost their jobs and face food shortages. This leads to social disruption and instability that can explode in social unrest.

Water supplies

Population pressures also result in potable water running short, as was vividly illustrated in mid-2018 when Cape Town, with a population of 4.5 million, was on the verge of running out of water. In 2015 Sao Paulo's 21.7 million people had fewer than twenty days water supply left, resulting from a drought caused by the destruction of the Amazonian rainforest effecting the rainfall cycle. The threat to the Amazon remains, particularly under the far-right government of Jair Bolsonaro in Brazil. Other large cities effected by water shortages include Beijing and India's Bangalore whose water supplies are already polluted. Egypt, which is dependent on the Nile River, Jakarta, Moscow, Istanbul and even London could face similar water shortages by 2025. Miami's groundwater supplies from the Biscayne Aquifer are already polluted by sea water. The city has a population of 2.7 million.

In fact, groundwater sources across the world are under enormous pressure, especially from irrigation for agriculture and food production. Worldwide, 30% of all freshwater is groundwater. Most of this is in porous, permeable rock and in open cavities and caves. Usage of this water for agriculture lowers groundwater levels and it will take centuries to replenish. Research published in *Nature* in 2017 showed that 11% of non-renewable groundwater was used in supplying the international food trade.[59] Much of the remainder was used in domestic food production. The three worst offenders in the use of groundwater for producing food for export are Pakistan (a big exporter of rice), India and the US. The crops that rely on non-renewable groundwater are wheat, rice, sugar, cotton and maize. The simple reality is that if groundwater supplies in food producing countries runs out, then large swathes of the world population will be facing starvation. Climate change has already thrown the world hydrological cycle out of its previous patterns, changing when rain falls, where it falls, and how much of it falls.

Fresh water is unevenly distributed across the world and regions facing water scarcity, many of them with big populations, are the western US, northern Mexico, Spain, Portugal, parts of North Africa, Saudi Arabia, South Africa, large parts of Australia, Pakistan, parts of northern and south-eastern India and the Andes region of South America. All of the evidence points to water shortages increasing with the result that around two billion people already lack access to safe water supplies.

Another issue linked to water shortages is the impact of the escalating demand for biofuels. Governments in Europe, the UK, the US and elsewhere are encouraging the use of greenhouse friendly fuels derived from plants to produce renewable energy. But producing such grains consumes huge amounts of water. A tonne of wheat, for instance, needs fifty tonnes of water, much of it coming from irrigation. At the same time in order to plant more crops, rainforests, which are very effective carbon sinks, are being cleared in many developing countries to grow grain for food and to supply the biofuel industry. This crazy, vicious circle vividly illustrates the set of contradictions that we face as a result of overpopulation and environmental destruction. Politicians, decision makers and even the general public simply don't seem to be able to make rational connections between things. Sadly, this matrix of interconnected and intractable problems will not be solved easily.

A 'sustainable' population

If population increase in developing countries is due to natural growth, what increase there is in first world countries comes from immigration. When you combine immigration with natural growth you get the overall growth rate: in the US it is 0.97, in Canada 0.90 and in the UK 0.42. Australia is an interesting example of a developed country with a very high overall growth rate, largely due to immigration. Its resident population at the beginning of 2019 topped twenty-five million. The country had a population growth rate of 1.6 in 2017, down from 2.19 in December 2008. However, 63% of Australia's growth rate comes from immigration. This means that natural increase (the excess of births over deaths) contributed only 37% to Australia's population increase. This level of immigration will have a very large impact on Australia's attempt to cut greenhouse gas emissions, because so many of the immigrants are coming from countries with a much lower standard of living and therefore a much lower contribution to global warming. These kinds of disconnections in policy formulation occur largely because immigration and population policies have become confused. Because pro-growth advocates quickly resort to calling anyone a 'racist' or 'nativist' who questions immigration on population grounds, these issues have become taboo topics among politicians and decision makers. They simply fail to see, or are unwilling to tackle, the mutual contradictions imbedded in their policies. Global warming, environmental destruction and loss of biodiversity vanishes between the discontinuities.

Although there is a fair amount of intra-European migration, most European Union countries have very low growth rates and some have moved into the negative zone. For instance, Russia's over-all population growth rate stands at -0.51, Lithuania at -0.53, Romania at -0.45, the Czech Republic at -0.03, Croatia at -0.09, Germany at -0.07, Poland at -0.15 and Italy at 0.13. It is interesting that some predominately Catholic countries like Italy, Lithuania, Poland and Croatia have now moved into negative population growth and the same is true of several Islamic countries. Thus, the caricatured clichés of the secular commentariat that Catholicism and Islam are uncritically supportive of high fertility are wrong. Reality is always more complex and rarely conforms to caricatures

Even if we could get a discussion on overpopulation started, how are we going to set ethical limits to human numbers? Some say that living 'sustainably' will achieve this. The usual definition of sustainability comes from the 1987 UN report *Our Common Future*, sometimes called the Brundtland Report after Norwegian prime minister, Gro Harlem Brundtland who chaired the UN Commission on development and environment. The report concluded that 'Sustainable development is development that meets the needs of the present without compromising the ability of future generations to meet their own needs'. This will be achieved, the report says, by the realization of seventeen sustainable development goals by 2030. These aim to eradicate 'poverty in all its forms and dimensions', so that 'no one will be left behind'. The report calls for safeguarding ecological sustainability, satisfying basic human needs and maintaining intergenerational equity.[60]

Brundtland didn't side-step population issues; the word is mentioned many times in the report, but the report admits it's an enormously difficult issue. It found that questions of population immediately plunged you into a morass of often unbridgeable attitudes focusing around culture, religion, regions, philosophies and social divisions. In the end, the Report's most serious limitation is its anthropocentric focus and its almost exclusive emphasis on human needs. It also delinks development and sustainability from population growth. It reflects the time it was written, the late-1980s, when ecological issues, biodiversity loss and global warming had not really impacted.

Nevertheless, following Brundtland there has been much debate about so-called 'sustainable population'. Many argue that it is not so much a question of absolute numbers, but inflated standards of living. The idea is that you can increase population size as long as you are able to rein-in excessive consumption. While it is true, as social justice advocates argue, that we refuse to recognize the unsustainable nature of our current lifestyle in developed countries, that is a separate issue from excessive numbers of people.

But this talk about sustainability is now irrelevant because world population is *already* unsustainable, with far too many people on earth. Numbers have to drop very significantly from the present high of 7.9 billion for any difference to be made in terms of threats to the environment and biodiversity, let alone to deal with global warming. The depopulation crisis faces us now, not in 2030, or 2050, let alone in 2100.

Carrying capacity

So, what is the earth's carrying capacity? How many people can it sustain while maintaining a reasonable standard of living, at the same time protecting biodiversity and dealing with global warming?

The UK-based think tank Population Matters has calculated various countries' carrying capacity by comparing their actual population numbers with how many people they could sustain with a 'modest footprint carrying capacity'. They define this as a lifestyle broadly related to European standards of living with a reduction of about three-fifths of present consumption of fossil fuels. Even by this standard they show that most countries are already living far beyond their carrying capacity. For example, the UK's mid-2021 population was 68.2 million with a light footprint capacity of 23 million, the US with 333 million has a sustainable capacity for 254 million, Australia, with 25.7 million, has a light footprint carrying capacity of 18 million. Israel has 8.7 million with a capacity for one million, and Italy with 60.3 million has a capacity for 16 million. Among developing countries China's 2020 population was 1.44 billion with a carrying capacity of 168 million, India had 1.39 billion with a capacity for 103 million, and Egypt with 104 million had a capacity for four million. Among the poorest nations Bangladesh has 166.4 million with a capacity for six million; Nigeria has 211.6 million with a capacity for ten million and Pakistan 225.4 million with a capacity for 26 million.[61] If we calculate the total numbers for just the countries mentioned, their carrying capacity is approximately 630 million, but their actual population is 4.3 billion.

Looking at this on a world-wide scale: if 7.9 billion people in 2021 is already too many, what is an optimal population size for the earth? This is the number of people that earth can sustain at a reasonable living standard for all without increasing global warming and biodiversity loss. But the definition of 'reasonable' is much debated and includes many variables. In a 1994 study G.C. Daily and Anne and

Paul Ehrlich focus on sufficient resources for people to enjoy freedom, human rights, culture, education, intellectual development while, at the same time, preserving biodiversity and ecosystems. Their estimates for an optimum world population size are somewhere between 1.5 and two billion people.[62] Other estimates are around 3.5 billion. The Australian Academy of Science found that a small majority of some sixty-five studies on how many people constitute a sustainable world population says that the earth's capacity is at or below eight billion. Thirteen of these studies says that the earth's carrying capacity is four billion or less.[63]

The mathematician Joel E. Cohen, having asked the question in his book *How Many People Can the Earth Support?* declines to answer because, he says, it all depends on how people live their lives.[64] An Indian ascetic or a Catholic monk or nun consume far less resources than a two-child nuclear family living in an over-sized house in a developed country. What is clear is that with the present population we are already well beyond the earth's biocapacity, that is human consumption is out-stripping the world's regenerative ability. This has been so since the early-1970s; at present we are chewing-up one and a half earths as we exploit the world's reserves. For instance, on 29 July 2019 we had already consumed all the natural resources available for that year and for the next five months we lived on credit. As recently as 2000, Earth Overshoot Day fell in October. At this rate we will be using two earths by 2030 and by 2050 we will consume three earths per year.

There may be a clue to a manageable world population number in the fact that up until the early-1070s we were not exceeding the ecological footprint of the planet. The world population then was 3.7 billion which is a bit less than half the present population. So perhaps we can say that around three billion is a manageable number. But it's not just numbers. Those concerned with human rights and equity of distribution constantly repeat that the problem is the scale and nature of consumption of resources by wealthy nations, an argument summed-up by the well-known Gandhi quotation: 'The world has enough for everyone's need, but not enough for everyone's greed.' The problem is that the Mahatma died in January 1948 when the world population was 2.4 billion; it is now more than three times that number. The difficulty facing this call for equality of distribution and lowering of living standards is that it is very difficult for democratic governments in developed countries to persuade their citizens to live simply and consume less, when their entire economies are based on the myth of infinite growth. In addition, the social justice tradition tends to idealize the poor. It assumes that once they are lifted out of poverty, they would not be as grasping and selfish as people in developed Western countries. It's as though lowering the standards of the rich countries and raising those of poor countries would lead to everyone meeting in the middle at a happy, sustainable level. Unfortunately, we humans are usually not that altruistic.

With the majority of studies saying that eight billion is the earth's outer limit carrying capacity – which I maintain is already *far* too high – with 7.9 billion now we are already in an unsustainable situation. So even if rich countries lowered their standard of living and the poor attained a modest lifestyle, the earth's carrying capacity would still be far exceeded. This indicates that unless development goals for third world countries, notions of equity, social justice and the abandonment of excessive consumer life-styles are inextricably linked to a serious reduction in human numbers, the situation we face remains impossible. While equity for the poorer nations is essential, we will just be whistling in the wind until we reduce human numbers to a sustainable level.

The only conclusion that we can come to is that Greta Thunberg is absolutely right. Addressing the UN Climate Action Summit 2019, the young Swedish women told politicians and national leaders: 'People are suffering, people are dying, entire ecosystems are collapsing. We are at the beginning of a mass extinction and all you can talk about is money and fairy tales of eternal economic growth. How dare you!' Something must be done and what I aim to do in the next chapter is to develop a principle that puts earth first.

6

Earth First

The cosmic perspective

We now come to the core argument of the book where I propose that the most basic moral principle governing all our behaviour is that the earth and the natural world must come first, before everything else. This needs to be strongly emphasized as we face the fact that there are *already* far too many of us, no matter what technophiles, pro-growth fantasists, or wishful-thinking demographers, or economists say.

We are in a unique situation and have never faced a challenge like this before because we've never had so many people on earth and it touches us personally and intimately in terms of children, family and our sense of individual continuity. It conjures up anxieties about our identity as persons, about our central position in the universal scheme of things, and our right to fertility and self-perpetuation. It also confronts our deeply ingrained religious, moral and spiritual beliefs and aspirations. It also questions the profoundly held, but largely unconscious assumption that we alone constitute the ultimate meaning of the earth and its creatures.

However, we will be unable to take on, let alone deal with the problem of population, if we are unwilling to move beyond our anthropocentric presuppositions and articulate a new, basically earth-centred and bio-centric moral foundation. We will have to be humble enough to jettison the notion that we somehow constitute the entire purpose and meaning of everything. Once we move beyond that, we will be able to adopt and integrate a new foundational moral principle based on the value and centrality of the whole of creation, not just on a presupposition about our own importance.

A way to grasp the fundamental reality of our real human situation in the cosmos and the absurdity of thinking that we somehow constitute the ultimate meaning of it all, is to reflect on the massively expanded horizons of time and space that modern astronomy and astrophysics have revealed to us. Anthropocentrism was understandable when we thought that the earth was the centre of the universe. In a sense we are still unconsciously struggling with the Copernican principle which replaced ancient earth-centric notions. No wonder Copernicus and Galileo scandalized their contemporaries whose entire cosmology was constructed on the notion that we are the unique centre of everything.

Astronomy and astrophysics have enormously expanded our vision of reality. Our Milky Way galaxy is about 100,000 light years across. Dwarfing that, estimates of the diameter of the observable universe is about ninety-three billion light years, but that is only what we can ascertain with our present instrumentation and calculations. With only five per cent of the universe visible to us, what we experience is only a tiny part of reality. We now speculate that the rest of space is made up of about seventy per cent dark energy and twenty-five per cent dark matter. At time of writing, we have little or no idea of what these realities are, except that they are a kind of fluid energy that strongly suggest that the theory of an ever-expanding universe might well be correct. I mentioned the Milky Way: astronomers estimate this galaxy has about one hundred billion stars, just one of which is our sun. It's estimated that there are about 100 billion galaxies out there, each with approximately 100 billion stars, all of them hurtling through space at gargantuan speeds. Of course, these figures are speculative, but there is no doubt that we live in a massive universe and the notion that we constitute it's meaning is just silly.

Also, our notion of time has expanded extraordinarily over the last cenntury. The cosmos has been in the process of evolution since the Big Bang approximately 13.8 billion years ago. Our earth began evolving about 4.5 billion years ago, yet our hominid ancestors have only been around for 300,000 years and modern humankind for about 160,000 years. In this time context how could we possibly imagine that we constitute the ultimate purpose of even the earth, let alone the cosmos? 'Here we are, born yesterday,' Thomas Berry says.[65] Modern astronomy, astrophysics and the history of the cosmos simply demand that we articulate an entirely new cosmological understanding of our humble place in reality. Linked to this will be a new approach to morality based on a fundamental, non-negotiable moral principle that removes humankind from being the central focus of ethics and shifts us into the much broader context of the cosmos, the absolute priority of the earth, the natural world and all its species.

The fundamental principle

This brings us to the most important sentence in the book. *The core moral principle that governs every person and community and every human action and decision, is that the wonderful biological diversity of life, expressed in all its detail and species, as well as the maintenance of the integrity and good of the earth itself, must come first and take priority over everything else.*

This principle is unequivocal. The diversity and integrity of earth comes before human desires, wishes, ambitions, needs and benefits. Our lives, like those of all species, are not absolute, but relative to the good of the whole. We are part of the earth's biological diversity, genetically rooted in it and utterly dependent upon it for survival. We don't, and never have constituted the ultimate meaning of the planet, let alone the cosmos and we have no right to dominate the earth, or destructively exploit it. This means that individual human lives and particular human communities are not absolute; they must act within the context of the good of the whole earth community. Given our total dependence on this system and our complete inability to exist outside of it, to think or act otherwise is delusional. There can be no compromise to make this principle more palatable. If humankind is to have any future, then this principle must be accepted as normative for all moral and ethical human action. Otherwise, the future is going to be very bleak indeed.

This earth-first principle implies an ethical revolution not just for post-modern capitalist individualism, the structures of society and the whole modern economy, but even more so for the world's great religious traditions that place humankind at the centre of reality. The principle also shifts the emphasis from a both/and vision – both humankind and the environment – to a focus which gives the primary emphasis to the natural world. This doesn't invalidate traditional morality; rather it shifts the emphasis previously attached almost exclusively to humankind across to the material world. This will be a particularly difficult shift for a religion like Christianity, which has previously focused primarily on humankind.

One thinker who has consistently emphasized the absolute centrality of the natural world and its biodiversity is the US Catholic 'geologian', as he called himself, Thomas Berry. His interpretation of spirituality and religion begins with the world, and he says that everything must be judged in the light of our relationship to it. He shifts the focus of modern religion outwards, away from its anthropocentric preoccupation with the human and intrapsychic. He says that all human realities 'must now be judged primarily by the extent to which they inhibit, ignore, or foster a mutually enhancing human–earth relationship.'[66] He believes that contemporary religion has failed us comprehensively, because the central role of religion is to provide us with an interpretive pattern, a way of making sense of ourselves in relationship to the world and cosmos and that it is failing to do that. Berry points out that we are sensitive to suicide, homicide and genocide, but we commit biocide (the killing of the life systems of the planet) and geocide (the killing of the planet itself) with impunity because we have no morality to deal with it. Both law and morality must recognise biocide and geocide as sins, social evils and crimes, just like homicide and genocide. Those who destroy the earth and its living forms, for whatever purpose, must be held both morally and legally responsible.

Berry is particularly critical of Christianity which he sees as having failed utterly in dealing with the devastation of the planet. He emphasizes that if we lose our sense of rapport with nature, we lose our sense of the divine, because it is the cosmos that stimulates and nourishes our imaginations, and any diminishing of our sense of the natural world stifles our imaginations. Berry is equally critical of secularism and modern science, which have also failed to help us interpret the significance and meaning of the natural world. 'The supreme irony is that just at this moment when such expansive horizons of past, present and future have opened up, humankind is suddenly precipitated into an inner anxiety and even into a foreboding about ourselves and the meaning of it all. Unable to bear such awesome meaning, we reject ourselves as part of the world around us

… While primitive people … had a sense of the magnitude of human existence … we are beset by a sense of confusion and alienation … Contemporary people have no spiritual vision adequate for these new magnitudes of existence.'[67]

A difficult principle

Having articulated this principle, I must admit that I'm apprehensive, because it's so subversive, challenging and confronting, especially in an individualistic, relativistic era like ours. We live in a culture in which we have become obsessed with the self, with our hurts, feelings and opinions, to the extent that we have lost a sense of relationship with other people and above all a relationship with the non-human world.

We also find it very difficult to think about all-inclusive principles that are broadly binding on all peoples and cultures, like the principle I have outlined. The majority of thinkers today claim that all reality is relative and subjective and that the only truth that can be attained is what is true for each person or group. When that relativism descends to a kind of crass individualism, when *numero uno* is all that counts, as it does for many, then it is time to say that this attitude has become toxic. This kind of post-modern individualism is particularly subversive when trying to discuss population. It essentially reduces the human community to fragmented interest groups and individuals guided at worst by the struggle to survive, and at best by a kind of libertarian hedonism. It is responsible for the modern mythology that all of humanity's traditional points of reference, value judgments and religious principles can be deconstructed, so that individuals and coalitions of particular interest reign supreme by developing their own truth and values. Like Donald Trump, they think that what is right for them, *is* right for them, contrary facts and values notwithstanding. Post-modernism has become increasingly toxic in Western secular society as it deconstructs all general moral principles and reduces ethics to the values and interests of individuals and particular groups. By claiming that the good of the earth and all its species comes before everything else, I am asserting an all-inclusive, absolute moral principle that nowadays goes very much against the contemporary grain. In post-modern terms, it is a monumental meta-narrative and meta-narratives are not in favour.

Modern psychology doesn't help us much either. Since the late-nineteenth century, psychology's focus has been almost exclusively on the mental health, or curing the psychic dysfunction of individuals. It's almost as though the outside world doesn't really exist. Modern culture is caught-up in an intense subjectivity, almost a kind of narcissistic solipsism, a poisonous self-obsession. As Philip Rieff pointed out in 1966 in *The Triumph of the Therapeutic*, modernity has been besotted with what he calls 'the psychological person' as we descended deeper and deeper into self-analysis and the quest for self-realization.[68] This became a contemporary obsession with many and in this therapeutic world, self-realization replaced self-transcendence and self-management replaced the kind of self-discipline handed down through our religious traditions, as the way to achieve human fulfillment. As Rieff says, psychological man turned inward, pre-occupied with the maintenance, nurturance and management of the self. Much of contemporary psychology is still caught-up in individual subjectivity and generally fails to recognize the importance of a world beyond the intrapsychic.

Since the advent of social media, this focus on the self has been re-enforced by an on-line world where people have become obsessed with the subjective projection of their *personae*, almost to the exclusion of the exterior world. Through Facebook, Twitter, WhatsApp, WeChat, Instagram and other apps, we construct inflated and larger-than-life digital images of our idealized selves and put them out there for others to admire in what is unequivocally a narcissistic exercise. Twitter encourages us to think that our thoughts, feelings and instant opinions and biases are monumentally important and others need to hear them. The number of followers we have tells us how 'important' we are. Nowadays we have so many means of communication and so little of substance to say. The reality is that self-obsession and the construction of an idealized *persona* easily modulates into narcissism and certainly doesn't leave much time for genuine self-reflection on the reality of the wider world, let alone concern for the environment and biodiversity. Contemporary anthropocentrism has narrowed into an obsessive form of narcissistic individualism.

Over the last couple of hundred years philosophers have also contributed to embedding anthropocentric individualism in our culture. Philosophy since the seventeenth century has become besotted with the dynamics of human interiority. Who am I, how do I know I know, is there anything really 'out there', these have become the prevailing questions. As a result, Western culture has, as Thomas Berry says, become inextricably caught-up in and 'absorbed by the pathos of the human'.[69]

The problem for us is that, in contrast to the rest of sentient creation, we don't have any excuse for not seeing ourselves in a broader ethical perspective, because evolution has given us a more highly developed sense of self-consciousness than other sentient creatures. By this I mean not just a consciousness of oneself as a self as distinct from other selves but, more importantly, we have a consciousness of the self as part of the greater reality of the world around us. This is not to say that other sentient species, particularly animals, lack self-consciousness, but ours is highly developed with conscience and moral sensitivity, and this deprives us of any excuse to escape reflecting on the reality of our situation.

At the same time, a truly honest reflection on our situation in the world would help us recover a profoundly humble estimation of our significance as we see ourselves within the perspective of the cosmos. The principle that the earth, its species and biological diversity must come first, will require a radical, but certainly not impossible shift in our thinking to an earth-centric and bio-centric morality. But having said that, some pretty tough consequences follow, and it is to these that I will turn now.

7

The Tough Issues

The ethical practicalities

Having articulated the basic principle that should govern our behavior for the future and having looked at the kind of cultural individualism and intense preoccupation with the self that we will have to overcome in the process of accepting the priority of the earth and biodiversity, I will now turn to some of the specific issues that will arise as we begin implementing our basic moral principle. It's here that we get to the heart of the matter: the ethical practicalities we need to confront to deal with overpopulation, let alone initiate depopulation.

It's clear that serious mistakes were made in previous attempts to limit population growth, particularly in India with the Congress Party government's top-down approach and attempted widespread forced sterilization of the poor. However, the problem is that in endlessly repeating a litany of negatives concerning depopulation, we lose sight of the real problem: what 7.9 billion people are already doing to the natural world? The real challenge is how do reduce population in a humane and, for me personally, Christian way. How do you respect people while, at the same time, call out the social and religious obscurantism that prevails in many societies? This isn't going to be easy, and if that means I'm caricatured as a 'Malthusian Cassandra', then I'll happily wear that label if it moves us toward confronting these devilishly difficult problems.

The fundamental question here is the right to reproduce. Linked to this is a set of secondary questions: what limits can the community, local, national or international, place on the rights of couples and families to decide the number of children they have? And then there are programs like the one child policy in China: are they ethically acceptable? Is it racist, or chauvinistic, or consistent with social justice, for developed countries that have already achieved ZPG, to demand family planning and population control as a prerequisite for economic assistance to developing nations with growing numbers? How much respect should be given to social, cultural and religious practices that emphasize fertility, as in countries like Niger?

Taking the question of fertility first: the present worldwide average is 2.5 children per woman. Most regions are already at ZPG (2.1 children), or close to it. In Latin America it is 2.0 children per woman, 1.9 in North America, 2.1 in Asia, 1.6 in Europe and 1.8 in Australia. The focus of the problem is north Asia and Africa where, on average in 2020, women had 4.44 children. Here the lack of even primary education for girls, means they who have little or no control over their lives and fertility. As we've seen, kin, family, clan and religious systems are pushing women into having children, although in many places these children are born into extended relational networks that help in looking after off-spring.

Overwhelming evidence shows that the most effective way to lessen fertility is to educate and liberate girls and keep them in school for as long as possible, but in most parts of sub-Saharan Africa this is not happening. Economic development is also important in encouraging birth control, but the infrastructure to create the jobs is non-existent across much of Africa. Children are useful in agricultural and subsistence societies and in urban slums because of their ability to work. With high infant and child mortality, extra children are seen as an insurance policy. 'Children are economic assets in poor countries, not liabilities like their middle-class counterparts [in developed countries]', where they cost a small fortune to educate and maintain.[70] It's not that African governments oppose family planning; it's just that they show little enthusiasm for birth control, even though the governing elites use it themselves. As a result, family planning services and reproductive health have not been widely available to the rural poor. Some African countries are having some success with family planning, especially when governments take the lead to support the programs, but there is often a slow uptake of such services.

Having said that, we still have to answer the fundamental question: who decides family size? The couple themselves, or what might be termed the broader public interest? I have used the term 'public interest' rather than the word 'community' purposely, because if we asked local communities in Niger, or Kiribati, or elsewhere to decide, they would opt for more, not fewer children. I have also used 'public interest' because population increase concerns not just the couple or local community, but all of us because overpopulation anywhere ultimately impacts on everyone on earth, even just in terms of massive numbers of ecological refugees looking for safe havens. Because population is an issue that concerns everyone, all of us have a right to persuade and ultimately to put pressure on countries, regions, communities and individuals that don't comprehend, or refuse to face their population challenges.

A basic question is that of reproductive rights: is the decision to have one, two, or more children purely a decision for the couple? Or are there limits to these rights? Part of the answer must be the level of demand that every extra person imposes on local ecological and bioregional structures. To decide to have a child is not a purely subjective act by couples, or a woman. It involves broader social and environmental issues. Socially, the moral question is: can this child be nurtured, cared for and fed? Can the family and community support it? Environmentally, the moral question is: what demands will looking-after this child place upon the local ecology? Can these be met? Is there evidence that the particular area is already over-populated leading to environmental degradation? If the region's ecology is already compromised, what is the future prognosis for its ability to support more people?

Historically, across all cultures prior to the late-nineteenth century, fertility was encouraged by family, religion and state in order to maintain population numbers, to contribute to common well-being and to extend a community's ability to protect and extend its territory. Throughout most of human history the decision to have a child was a social act endowed with religious and ethical connotations. But with the advent of individualism and the dominance of the nuclear family in the developed Western world from the late-nineteenth century onwards, the notion has developed that reproduction is a purely private act in which the community and the state have no say. Having a child is seen as a purely private decision that fulfills and completes oneself and one's relationship.

What we need to recover is the sense that the right to have children belongs within the general context of the common good, broadly understood. Such a decision must be taken within the context of the ability of the couple, the community and the local environment to support the child. This decision must also be taken within the context of overpopulation and the rights of nature and other species. To be absolutely clear: I am saying that the right to reproduce is not just a subjective decision for a woman, or couple, or even a family, clan, or local community. To have a child is a social act that is contextualized by moral constraints focusing on the ability of both the couple and broader environment to support that child. In other words, I am resituating fertility in an ecological and social context where it properly belongs.

Slow down or stop?

But all of this really only deals with gradually slowing down population growth. We're already beyond the earth's physical carrying capacity and food and water shortages will soon become acute. The then-UN Secretary-General, Ban Ki-Moon, warned in 2008 that food production would have to rise by fifty per cent by 2030 to feed the world population. We might be able to achieve that if we approved genetically-modified crops, more irrigation and an even greater use of fertilizers and chemicals. But these imagined technological panaceas ignore the consequences of such actions: widespread loss of biodiversity, the collapse of river systems, land degradation, increasing salinity and widespread chemical pollution. Australia, a major world food producer, is already experiencing all of these problems.

Sure, we could eliminate all other species that are not useful for human survival and retain only those needed for food production and human needs. In that type of food-lot world we might physically survive, but what a dystopia it would be with no natural beauty, other species eliminated and every bit of fertile land turned over to industrial agriculture. It would be a monochrome world with nothing to stimulate our imaginations. Also, in terms of justice and equity, we have to think of our children and grandchildren who will inherit the mess that we have created. Inter-generational equity is becoming an increasingly important moral principle.

Beyond the individual right to reproduce is a set of difficult questions focusing on government imposition of family size. The prime example of this is the one child policy in China. Critics have condemned the policy as an infringement of the right of the couple to make these kinds of decisions, while ignoring the size of the problem the Communist government faced as it tried to lift people out of rural poverty. At first, there was an emphasis on late age of marriage, longer intervals between births and smaller families. Then, in 1979, the one child policy was imposed, which was relatively easy to do in a one-party state. Even with this policy, China's population still increased from 1.07 billion in 1980 to 1.4 billion in 2020, although some experts think there might be about 90 million fewer people in China than the official figure. In 1979 Chinese women had 2.91 children. By 2020 when the policy was eased, the fertility rate was 1.69. Critics of the policy are concerned about the social consequences, such as spoilt, selfish only children, imbalances between boys and girls, the skewed support ratio between the working age population and the elderly, the breakdown of family and kin ties, forced abortions of second children, and what one article quaintly describes as 'three decades of abnormal sex'.[71]

Interestingly, despite the lifting of the of the one child restriction, many Chinese couples are still choosing to have a single child and this looks set to continue into the future because the one child policy lifted the living standards of many young Chinese. What Western critics of the policy miss are that the problems they cite are really social and psychological problems. They forget that the policy aimed at getting people out of poverty and lessening the impact of overpopulation on the environment.

Given the situation we're in at present with our excessive numbers already impacting destructively on nature and biodiversity, some direct form of government action is required to encourage people to limit the number of children they have, even in developed democracies, difficult as this will be. Where there is a failure to do this voluntarily, some form of limitation of human freedom may be justified. It may not be as draconian as in China, but governments do have a moral obligation, especially in developing countries, to intervene and confront destructive social and religious policies favoring high rates of fertility. It's a matter of balancing two unpalatable realities: government intervention to control fertility and limits on individual freedoms; or the much worse chaos that will inevitably result from overpopulation in a particular region because of a failure to act. It is a choice of the lesser of two evils.

There is at least one proven way of decreasing population and that is late age of marriage. Historically, one place where this has successfully occurred is Ireland. The background is that because of land arrangements, from about 1770 onwards, Irish peasants married in their late teens, leading to high fertility and a rapid increase in population. Most Irish were living in desperate poverty and the population went from 3.19 million in 1754, to 6.8 million in 1821, reaching a peak of 8.1 million in 1845. Then in years 1845–1846 the potato blight struck, resulting in a major crop failure. The vast majority of the Irish poor depended on potatoes as a staple food, and the blight led to famine. British relief attempts were badly disorganized and at least one million people died and another million emigrated to North America, Australia and elsewhere. Influenced by Malthus' ideas, this disorganization was part of a deliberate policy of British government bureaucrats to reduce 'surplus population'.

The Irish census of 1851 showed that the population had dropped to 6.55 million, a decrease of almost two million in six years. After that, and especially after independence from Britain in July 1921, the 'Irish population continued to decrease … bottoming out in the 1960s when only slightly more than half as many people lived on the island as had lived there 120 years previously', that is just over four million.[72] The primary reason for this depopulation was late age of marriage. People in rural Ireland postponed marriage until enough land became available to support a new family. Usually only one son inherited the land, with his siblings heading overseas to find a life elsewhere, or remaining home but never marrying, or joining a religious order, or entering the priesthood. 'Few rural populations have ever resorted to what Malthus called "prudential restraint" so fiercely or so completely as the Irish did after the famine.'[73] This was underpinned by a puritanical form of Catholicism that emphasized sexual repression. You might criticize the Irish church for this, but at least it radically depopulated the country and saved people from the appalling poverty of pre-famine Ireland. The population of the whole island was 6.8 million in 2021, almost the same as the population in 1851, and 1.3 million less than in 1845.

Another way of slowing population growth, especially in developed countries, is to limit health over-servicing for older people, with some of those resources being re-directed to the developing world, especially in terms of family planning and reproductive health. Before anyone rushes in to accuse me of supporting eugenics, let me say that I'm almost 81 at the time of writing and I only support euthanasia when people are already close to death, in acute pain and freely choose this option. But I am saying that the processes of nature should be allowed to take their course and that any form of *extraordinary* medical intervention to keep people alive who are over, say, seventy-five, should be ruled out. By 'extraordinary' here I mean disproportionate or burdensome interventions, often against the patient's expressed desires, to keep people alive when it is clear that their quality of life has declined. My view is that reasonable care should be taken, which means the benefit of treatments being proportionate to the burdens they impose. The important general principle here is that nature should be allowed to take its course and that savings achieved through limiting over-servicing of older people in the developed world should be redirected to family planning in the developing world.

Liberating girls and women

The pivotal issue in population decrease in Ireland was delayed marriage, supported by religion, economic constraints and emigration. The situation we face today in developing countries is more complex than in a single culture like Ireland, strongly united by a common faith. Nowadays achieving late age of marriage is more difficult in places like sub-Saharan Africa, but at least policies can be introduced to make sure that girls are not married early and that they are given time to complete their education, at least until the end of secondary school, or preferably later. This is a key area where Western governments should be focusing their aid, because with a secondary education, women would be freer to make their own decisions about marriage and fertility. Family planning, contraception and reproductive health programs must also be readily available to them.

Child marriage in Africa is condemned by the Maputo Protocol of 2003. However, many African countries have ignored the Protocol and child marriage remains widespread. We've already seen in Niger that early marriage contributes enormously to high fertility. You can see the same across much of sub-Saharan Africa with girls in neighboring Burkina Faso married on average at 17.9, Chad at 16, Guinea at 16.5 and Sierra Leone at 17 years. Many of these girls are simply not prepared physically or emotionally for motherhood. They drop out of school, are desperately poor and often experience spousal and family violence, especially if they are taken into their husband's households. Their poverty and marginalization are passed on to their children.

All of the evidence from WHO, UNESCO and OECD support the notion that the status and education of women is centrally important in fertility control. When they are educated at least to the end of high school and have property rights, fertility rates drop. This is borne out in countries like Cuba, China, Thailand and the South Indian state of Kerala, where women have an education, some economic independence and the right to inherit property. In order to encourage developing countries to adopt a program of freedom for girls and women to realize their potential, aid should be contingent not only on providing family planning, but also on programs of education for girls and women. Legal and social structures need to be introduced that liberate them from oppressive patriarchal and familial structures.

We already know that the education and liberation of women, government supported family planning, reproductive health, educating men in responsible fertility, all work effectively. The evidence is overwhelming that the higher the level of education that a girl or woman attains, the fewer children she will have. Education takes her out of the family and clan situation where her only worth is derived from bearing children, delays marriage until she has some maturity and gives her confidence in controlling her fertility. This has been borne-out in Ethiopia, the second-most populated country in Africa after Nigeria. Since 1994 the country has expanded its education system and this has helped to lower fertility rates, but with 40% of Ethiopia's population under the age of fifteen, the population is still estimated to increase from 117 million in 2021 to 191 million by 2050.

Successes in improving the lot of women have meant that between 1950 and 2020 the worldwide total fertility rate has dropped from 5.05 to 2.44. In developing countries, the rate has been reduced, on average, from six to three births per woman. If we take the period 1950 to 2020 fertility rates in Mexico have dropped from 6.7 to 2.4, in Peru from 6.9 to 2.27, and in Indonesia from 5.4 to 2.32. I mention these countries because Peru and Mexico are nominally Catholic and Indonesia is the largest Islamic country in the world. Both Catholicism and Islam are often criticized for their opposition to contraception and abortion. Catholics get blamed for their failure to confront the population problem in Latin America, Africa, the Pacific and the Philippines where, despite hierarchical opposition to birth control, the fertility rate has decreased from an extraordinary high of 7.4 in 1950 to 2.58 in 2020, showing that Catholics generally follow their consciences and the social reality in which they live regarding contraception. In fact, despite hierarchical condemnation, research shows that 'the majority of couples in predominantly Catholic and Islamic countries use contraception.'[74]

Population control programs need to emphasize that men must also be held accountable for fertility. They should be encouraged to support their wives and partners in getting an education and work outside the home. They should also be morally and legally pressured to get a vasectomy after a second or third child. The 'snip' is a non-intrusive, simple procedure that is common in developed countries and is an extremely effective means of contraception that doesn't diminish sexual desire and fulfillment. However, in developing countries, particularly in machismo cultures, men are ignorant of the procedure, or if they know about it, they incorrectly equate it with castration and impotence, rendering them unable to work. Female sterilization is much more common in developing countries, but the moral and legal onus needs to be re-focused on men, making them accept responsibility for fertility. Education programs also need to be introduced that aim at educating men out of the notion that the number of children they have is a sign of virility and masculinity. So-called 'machismo' is really a form of toxic misogyny. The great strength of urban living is that once family planning, educational and medical services are provided, people, particularly men, can be put under pressure by the community and influential others to change their attitudes and use these facilities. An important role that churches and religions could and should play in patriarchal, honor/shame type societies is educating boys and men to respect women's freedom and basic rights. The fact that parts of Mediterranean Latin-Italian culture is still dominated by machismo after almost two millennia of Catholicism points to the complete failure of the church in instill genuine Christian values.

The depopulation option

But everything we've said so far is about limiting numbers, rather than depopulation. With a world population of 7.9 billion, we are already so far beyond a sustainable relationship with nature that we must begin to reduce our numbers now, not hope for some kind of future levelling-out out. The key contemporary question we face is: can present population trends be modified in the short term to *reduce* numbers? Is depopulation possible? The truth is most demographic experts would answer 'no' to that question. The distinguished demographer, Gilles Pison of the Paris Museum of Natural History, is blunt. 'It would be unrealistic,' he says, 'to imagine that population trends can be modified over the short term. Depopulation is not an option.' He points out that 'Even if world fertility were just 1.6 children per women, as is [already] the case in Europe and China, the population would continue to increase for several more decades; there are still large numbers of adults of childbearing age who were born when fertility was still high, so the number of births also remains high.'[75] In a careful analysis Pison shows that short of nuclear war, or a massive natural catastrophe, or an horrendous pandemic, demographic inertia will prevent immediate depopulation. Others, like Daniel Bricker and John Ibbitson, argue that world population will peak at nine billion by 2060, much earlier than the UN and other experts predict, and then rapidly decline, so that the issue post-2060 will be a fast-shrinking population rather than an expanding one.[76]

However, prediction is an inexact science and the issue of depopulation calls for lateral thinking and recognizing that despite all our statistical projections, we must always allow that serendipity, or an unexpected change out of left field, can occur. COVID-19 is an example of that. We've also seen some of the practical measures we can take without imposing draconian measures on people. Some of these are: universal, free access to contraception, reproductive health and appropriate sex education for all young people, as well as funding education for girls at least to the end of secondary school. Governments should end subsidies and incentives that reward people for having extra children and, in fact, those who have more than three children should incur a tax penalty, particularly in developed countries. We've seen that almost all countries are over-populated in terms of their sustainable carrying capacity when assessed against a 'modest footprint carrying capacity'.

Nevertheless, Pison is right when he says that short of nuclear war, or a massive natural catastrophe, or horrendous pandemic, it will be natural processes that impose depopulation on humankind. For instance, given the rate at which we are pumping carbon dioxide into the atmosphere, we are making the near-future exceptionally uncertain and unpredictable for ourselves, because increasing temperatures could easily result in the unexpected early arrival of a 'hothouse climate', a tipping point at which temperatures might well escalate 5°C, resulting in sea level rises of ten or more meters. We simply can't discount such an event. It would certainly make depopulation a reality.

Also, if there is one thing which COVID-19 has taught us, it is an awareness of pandemics. They are not new; they have always been with us. Just taking the last two thousand years in the European region, pandemics have recurred regularly, with the most horrendous one being the Black Death, which peaked in Europe from 1347 to 1351. It spread extraordinarily quickly through Asia, the Middle East and Europe, after originating in China in the mid-1330s. Reliable estimates say that it killed more than fifty per cent of Europe's population, spreading either via mosquitoes, or directly from person to person.[77] The Black Death occurred early in the Little Ice Age, a period lasting from the late-1200s until the early-nineteenth century, which took hold mainly in the northern hemisphere. Its causes were complex and resulted in animal diseases, drought, famine, recurrent plague and a human population under considerable economic and social pressure.

Another well-known historic pandemic was the so-called 'Spanish Flu', the influenza outbreak of 1918–1919. Although there is some debate as to where this particular H1N1 strain of flu originated, it was first observed in an army camp in the US state of Kansas and it spread rapidly at the end of the First World War.[78] Coming in three waves, almost 500 million were infected and more than 50 million died. Most of those infected were young, healthy adults under the age of forty.[79] This pandemic was particularly bad in India where as many as eighteen million people died.

With COVID-19, pandemics have re-emerged into public consciousness. But it's not the first zoonotic virus that has spread from bats via an intermediate animal to humans. The earlier Coronavirus, SARS-CoV, which originated in China's Yunnan province in late-2002, spread human to human through coughing, sneezing and other forms of physical contact.[80] SARS was less infectious than COVID-19, but it had a higher mortality rate. Its Middle Eastern variant, MERS-CoV, killed half of the people infected by it. Because of the small numbers infected, SARS was quickly forgotten, only to return in COVID-19, which also originated in bats, transferring through an intermediary animal, in Wuhan, Hubei Province, China in late-2019. It is not unusual for viruses to jump species and the interconnected world that we inhabit today is ideal for viruses to seek new hosts. The initial animal-to-person infection then spread person-to-person. The Delta strain of the virus is much more infectious and without vaccination we have no immunity to it.

What is interesting about COVID-19 is that its first major outbreaks were in developed countries like the US, the UK and Western Europe where people are much more likely to travel, spreading the disease in the process. New York City is an example of this: it is a melting pot with eight million inhabitants and over fifty million visitors each year, all cramming into an area of 480 square kilometers. The inter-connected nature of the contemporary world makes it inevitable that contagious pandemics are going to spread, especially in cities and regions where locals and tourists come together. At the time of writing the Delta strain had spread in the developed and developing world with particular impacts in India, Brazil and Indonesia. At first Africa seemed less effected by COVID-19, but by mid-2021 the disease was spreading, especially in South Africa where there had been some 2.1 million cases and more than 64,000 deaths. WHO director general,

Tedros Adhanom Ghebreyesus, said that the spread of Coronavirus in Africa 'is driven by a mix of public fatigue, social mixing, ineffective use of public health and social measures, and vaccine inequity, and the spread of new variants.'[81] With weak health systems, the threat of COVID-19 remains.

What COVID-19 and the more lethal variants remind us of is our sheer vulnerability to pandemics, resulting from our constant interference with the basic rhythms of nature. We have already seen this with viruses like Ebola, HIV-AIDS and Zika virus which are also zoonotic. The natural host for HIV-AIDS, for example, are chimpanzees, and the virus passed from these animals to humans through the consumption of bush meat, or contact with animal blood, probably in the 1920s, completely unnoticed by medical authorities. The first known cases were diagnosed in the early-1960s, spreading to the West in the 1970s through unprotected sex with infected people in the Democratic Republic of Congo. Up to one hundred million people have died of HIV-AIDS since it first emerged, most of them in Africa, with the death-rate peaking in 2005. Another zoonotic virus is Ebola which breaks out periodically in West Africa. In 2015–2016 in Guinea, Liberia and Sierra Leone, it killed 11,325 people and infected 28,600. It almost certainly originated through contact with fruit bats. Forms of avian influenza, that is infections that cross from birds to humans, can also cause severe illness through contact, usually with poultry.

According to Edward Holmes there is only one way to curb the emergence of new zoonotic diseases: we need to reduce human interaction with wild animals, close wet markets, stamp out the illegal wildlife trade and increase research into animal populations that carry coronaviruses.[82] Here it is worth noting that international trade in wild animals and their sale in wet markets not only inflict appalling cruelty on the animals involved, but also reflect a complete disrespect for nature and our fellow creatures. These markets are not confined to China, but are also common in Vietnam, Indonesia and other parts of Asia. Because this trade is very lucrative, it tends to be dominated by criminal syndicates utterly without scruple, or concern for animal welfare.

A related source of pandemics are the massive agribusinesses that clear-fell whole areas of tropical forest to plant harvestable crops like palm oil, soybeans, or to establish cattle ranches. An example of this is the on-going destruction of the Amazon rainforest in Brazil, or widespread forest destruction in Borneo, Papua-New Guinea and Solomon Islands. Not only do some of the world's most endangered animals and plants live in these forests, but with some five million hectares clear-felled every year, these massive landscape dislocations place people in much closer contact with wild animals – primates, bats and rodents – that carry dangerous pathogens. Destructive clear-felling also leads to flooding that breeds mosquitos and eliminates the birds and amphibians that kept mosquito numbers down. This, in turn, can lead to the spread of diseases like malaria, dengue fever, Zika and other viruses. Factory farming of chickens, pigs and other domestic animals also provides the ideal locus for the development of other deadly pathogens, such as variations on the flu virus, E. coli, campylobacter which can lead to gastroenteritis, salmonella which infects humans from poultry and BSE, or mad cow disease. Again, aside from the appalling cruelty inflicted on animals in these industrial conditions, factory farming may well be the source of the next pandemic.

COVID-19 reminds us that pandemics are a constant reality in human history and that nature uses them as a way of restoring balance when one species is out of balance with the whole. Sure, in comparison to the Black Death or the flu pandemic of 1918–1919, it's a relatively gentle reminder, at least at the time of writing in mid-July 2021 when there were 187,519,800 confirmed cases of COVID-19, including 4,050,400 deaths.

In a sense, pandemics and wars seem to have become less important, simply because nowadays there are so many people. An illustration of this is the period 1900 to 1930 which includes World War I and the flu pandemic. In 1900 the world population was 1.6 billion. Despite some 15 to 20 million military and civilian deaths in the First World War and probably more than 50 million deaths in the flu pandemic, the world population in 1920 was 1.86 billion and by 1930 it was over two billion. The fact is that even this death rate was a mere blip on the population increase graph.

However, we should not underestimate nature's ability to scale-up to meet the size of the threat. We should not deceive ourselves that our massive interference with and manipulation of the natural world won't stimulate a response. COVID-19 may just be the pandemic overture to a much greater tragedy, because in the end nature won't be mocked. Depopulation is an unavoidable imperative, whether we do it willingly and responsibly ourselves, or we let nature do it for us. Our numbers are unsustainable and nature is a self-correcting system that will not be mocked.

And it may not be a pandemic that puts us in our place. Another threat facing human fertility is the decline in the quantity and quality of male sperm, especially in developed Western countries. Research over the last fifty years has shown that sperm counts for men from North America, Europe, Australia and New Zealand have dropped by 59.3% since 1973.[83] Also, the mobility of sperm, that is their ability to get to the fallopian tube to fertilize an egg, has also dropped. If these declines continue, eventually many men will not be able to reproduce naturally. This decrease in sperm numbers and motility might point to an eventual reproductive collapse that could rapidly decrease population. Other analyses show a less marked decline in sperm concentration in Latin America and Asia over the last fifty years, although evidence from Africa indicates that from 1965 to 2015 there has been 'an overall 72.6% decrease in mean sperm concentration … in the past 50 years'.[84] Were this to continue, or a sudden catastrophic collapse occur in sperm counts, we would have a genuine chance of quickly lowering the rate of population increase. At present what we're dealing with is a downward trend that is probably caused by the variety of chemicals that have been released into the environment since the 1960s. The chemical components of plastic manufacture have been focused on as one possible cause, but attention has also centred on pesticides, heavy metals, as well as lifestyle causes like being overweight, high alcohol consumption, smoking, stress and a sedentary lifestyle. They have all probably contributed to sperm count problems.

Whatever way it occurs, I don't think we can avoid the inevitability of confronting depopulation and radically lessening our numbers. The alternative is the real danger of human extinction. I'm not alone in thinking this.

Frank Fenner's prognosis

Smallpox used to be one of the world's great killers. It's caused by another zoonotic virus, the variola virus. This can be traced back remotely to Egypt and later China, with it spreading to Europe in the seventh century AD. Smallpox was a devastating disease that killed three out of ten people who caught it and it disfigured and blinded many more. In an historical first for any disease, smallpox was finally completely eradicated worldwide in 1980. The distinguished Australian National University virologist, Professor Frank Fenner, was the man who led the program primarily responsible for the elimination of smallpox. In the last years of his long life – he died in 2010 aged ninety-five – I used to meet Frank reasonably often because we were both patrons of Sustainable Population Australia. We often discussed the problem of overpopulation on a global scale and how we might ascertain a sustainable carrying capacity for Australia.

A gentle, compassionate man, Frank told me that he had moments when he seriously doubted that he had done the right thing in helping to eliminate smallpox which, after tuberculosis, was probably the most lethal disease that humankind has ever experienced. However, he was proud that he had helped to relieve the suffering of those who had been infected; some 500 million people had died of the disease in the nineteenth century alone and 300 million in the twentieth century before smallpox's eradication. But as a medical doctor and scientist deeply concerned about the future of both the natural world and humankind, Frank felt ambivalent that he had helped to eliminate one of the ways that nature used to deal with human numbers, terrible as smallpox was. He was aware of the moral ambiguity embedded in the kind of research that tackles widespread diseases that keep population numbers in check. He understood that nature was impersonal and neutral, neither good nor bad, vindictive nor benevolent. It just was, and when things got out of balance, it sought equilibrium. His overwhelming concern was that overpopulation would lead to even more awful, painful and deadly diseases that would cause much more suffering. He was also very aware of our moral obligation to coming generations as we voraciously consume non-renewable resources and reduce biodiversity.

The self-questioning of such a truly distinguished scientist and humanitarian highlights the terrible moral conundrum facing us today. Understandably, we are doing our best to prevent pandemics, but it is pandemics and diseases that are the processes that nature uses to keep the living world in balance. This is the dilemma we face: how do you maintain the justifiable need to preserve human life when our out-of-control numbers are making such demands on the earth? Perhaps for most people this is not a question that enters their consciousness, and some will think it appalling to propose such a choice. From an anthropocentric perspective, especially in a crisis like COVID-19, the traditional position is that humankind comes before everything else and mainstream ethics supports that position. But if you posit the fundamental principle that the integrity of nature comes before everything else, including humankind, if you think that anthropocentrism and overpopulation will lead to a situation in which the world will become a bio-degraded, awfully inhospitable place, then at the very least you ought to be able to ask these kinds of questions. Of course, doctors will respond that they are bound by the Hippocratic Oath to care for patients and practice preventative medicine. No one is questioning that. But they are also bound to make sure that the balance of potential benefits outweighs the risks of harm. I'm the first to admit that these are very difficult and confronting ethical questions within traditional moral frameworks and I'm not sure that I have the answer. But given our present situation, we at least have to ask the questions.

So, in the end will any of this make any difference? Certainly, many think we are now well beyond even a massive pandemic making much difference to population numbers. Even if we had a catastrophic global pandemic that killed two billion people reducing the population to 5.8 billion, which was the world's population in 1990, this is still too many for the earth to sustain. Let's say three billion died; that's the world population in 1983, again probably still too many.

Besides pandemics, another situation in which many people die is that of famine, usually exacerbated by drought. An example is the Great Indian Famine of 1876–1878 in which some 5.5 million people died. At the time of writing some thirteen million people in the Horn of Africa are facing an acute food crisis due to drought and civil war in Ethiopia, and drought in northern Kenya and Somalia. Just across the Red Sea from the Horn of Africa is Yemen. The country has been war-torn for many years and at present is caught-up in a civil war with Saudi Arabia supporting the Sunni government against Shite Houthi rebels. The country has had food shortages for years, exacerbated by war and conflict. Despite this, the population has increased from 5.3 million in 1960 to about 30.5 million in mid-2021. The result is probably the worst humanitarian crisis on earth. About 17 million people are starving due to conflict, a collapsed economy and a failure of food distribution.

This leads to another difficult question: should people actually be living in such a marginal region as the Horn of Africa, with global warming going to make the situation there much worse than it already is? Can we justify trying to sustain people in this landscape when we know that supporting them there is only a short-term solution and that another worse drought will inevitably follow? Are external aid agencies compounding misery by supporting people with short-term aid when their long-term prognosis in a particular landscape is unsustainable? People feel good by responding to human suffering wherever they see it, but are you really helping by intervening in situations that in the end are intractable? David Attenborough says that nature is already sorting things out for us. He says that 'we keep putting on [TV] programs about famine in Ethiopia. [There are] too many people there. They can't support themselves – and it's not an inhuman thing to say … until humanity manages to sort itself out and get a coordinated view about the planet, it's going to get worse and worse.'[85]

Unpalatable as they are, if we don't ask these kinds of questions the consequences for the future of humankind and the planet will be terrible. We will be cursed by coming generations if we don't face facts now. In the last year of his life Frank Fenner expressed deep concern about the future, fearing that it was already too late for humankind. '*Homo sapiens* will become extinct,' he said, 'perhaps within 100 years. A lot of other animals will too. It's an irreversible situation.' He added: 'Mitigation [of human numbers] would slow things down a bit, but there are too many people here already.'[86] So here we are back at the seemingly intractable challenge: not just stabilizing numbers, but reducing them.

Yes, Frank Fenner and his fellow scientists were right to try to lessen human suffering and death by eliminating smallpox. But he also understood something that many today just don't get: that even in curing disease, we interfere with the rhythms of nature. The result: we can be certain that in regions where population numbers are still exploding, life will become increasingly intolerable.

Facing the facts

As we end this chapter, Dear Reader, I'm not sure that I've convinced you that we'll be able to *decrease* population, to depopulate, rather than just slowing its growth. I'm not even sure that I've convinced myself! Perhaps the pessimists are right; the path that we're on leads to the unavoidable conclusion that Frank Fenner was right when he said humankind will be gone sometime soon.

Many will argue that I have stated the choice facing us far too starkly, that we are not facing an either/or situation, that there is middle ground that can be reached. Yes, it's true that the problem we face is population multiplied by consumption, and that if we cut consumption in the developed world and lived more simply, then we might we be able to sustain 7.9 billion people more equitably. But there are two problems here. The first is that those who assert this never have to face the political cost and social backlash of deciding to cut living standards in developed, democratic countries. The second is that the poor in developing countries are not going to be satisfied with remaining where they are in terms of consumption. They will, understandably, want ever higher standards of living and will use increasing resources in the process of achieving that. Even if we could manage to achieve a fall in the living standards of developed countries, and somehow were able to raise those of developing countries, we won't have achieved anything. It's just that more people would have access to the same pie, and we're already eating almost a pie and a half each year.

The most important thing we have to realize is that we're in a totally new moral situation. Never before have we faced such a challenging choice, nor have we had to ask such hard questions. I would argue that many of the old moral principles no longer apply once you shift from an anthropocentric to an earth-biocentric ethic. Once you concede that humans are part of the earth system and totally dependent upon it, once you abandon the illusion that we somehow constitute the entire meaning of biological history, even cosmic history, then you begin to see humanity in another context. No longer is human life unequivocally absolute, but our relative importance is determined by our place in the scheme of earth history. Of course, our lives have value, but that value is not so total that other species have to be sacrificed to maintain it. What we need to recover is an earth-centric moral perspective and to see ourselves as part of nature, not over-and-against it.

In the end, if we are not prepared to confront the stark issue of human numbers and overpopulation, if we try to continue with the illusion that somehow the entire world can be sacrificed for the good of humankind, then we need to think long and hard about the world we will be leaving to our children and grandchildren, or, if you are still young, the world you might inherit as you age. Because the reality is that nature is responding to our contempt. There are just too many of us already and we are using up too many resources as we drive so many of our fellow creatures into extinction. We shouldn't be surprized that the world is responding.

Here Greta Thunberg can teach us something. Yes, she is still young and, yes, her communications skills might be a tad confronting for adults who take themselves too seriously. Thunberg says that she was depressed and overwhelmed before she began protesting about global warming outside Sweden's parliament in 2018, calling on school students across the world to seize the initiative. More than a million of them went on strike from classes in March–May 2019 in 110 countries and protested worldwide about global warming. It was only when she decided to take action that she began to experience a sense of hope. She says: 'The school-striking children, when I see them – that is very hopeful. And the fact is that people are very unaware of the climate crisis. I mean, people aren't continuing like this and not doing anything because they are evil, or because they don't want to. We aren't destroying the biosphere because we are selfish. We are doing it simply because we are unaware. I think that is very hopeful, because once we know, once we realise, then we change, then we act.'[87]

Thunberg told the UK House of Commons that we need what

she called 'cathedral thinking' that is we need to be like the builders of the great medieval cathedrals. We lay the foundation without knowing 'exactly how to build the ceiling'. She said she was sure that 'the moment we start behaving as if we were in an emergency, we can avoid climate and ecological catastrophe'. But we've got to start today. 'We have no more excuses.'[88] Thunberg must have touched a chord with people because she has been viciously attacked by the right-wing climate deniers, particularly in the Murdoch media, with comments on her 'immaturity and lack of experience', or even her mental health being questioned.

'Once we know, once we realise, then we change, then we act.' That's the key here. We have to refuse to surrender to a crippling sense of despair that no matter what we do, we will achieve nothing. We need the determination that we won't go down without a fight. US Congresswoman, Alexandria Ocasio-Cortez, agreed with Thunberg. She says: 'Hope is not something that you have. Hope is something that you create, with your actions. Once one person has hope, it can be contagious. Other people start acting in a way that has more hope.'[89] In other words, hope only really becomes hope when we begin to act on it.

8

Population and Biodiversity

Humans and biodiversity

All species are species-centric, so it's understandable that we care for those like ourselves. We are sensitive to the needs, feelings and pain of other people and reach out to them. But one of the worst aspects of our species-centrism is that we often don't extend that empathy to other sentient creatures with whom we share the planet. Sure, we experience a sense of fellow-feeling for animals we find attractive, especially domestic animals and pets. But we can be appallingly obtuse and totally ignore the suffering of wild animals, including the massacre of literally millions of them on our roads where they are often left to die in agony.

On an even vaster scale, wild animal species are under threat from habit destruction, invasive feral pests, pollution and above all climate change which will eliminate animals unable to adapt. We can't morally absolve ourselves of responsibility for the destruction of so many non-domestic animals, because it is the pressure of overpopulation that causes biodiversity loss. This most often begins with the destruction and elimination of food sources for these animals with the clearing of vegetation, forests and landscapes upon which they depend for survival. An example of this is the iconic Australian tree-dwelling marsupial, the koala, which is threatened by loss of habitat as land is cleared for housing, mining and agriculture.

We've already seen the loss of many larger animals at the top of the food chain with the impact of hunter-gatherers on the megafauna in pristine environments, as well as the consequences of the introduction of settled agriculture with wildlife losses continuing with the expansion of human settlement. For example, in the Nile Valley, elephants, giraffes and rhinoceroses had been driven from the landscape by the age of the pyramids around 2,350BC. As civilizations came and went in the Mediterranean basin, animals like lions and leopards disappeared, with the last of them becoming extinct in Greece by 200BC.

With early humans, animal extinctions were the unintended by-products of human expansion, but it was the Romans who were animal slaughterers on an industrial scale. There is something profoundly pathological about the way the mostly upmarket audience in places like Rome's Coliseum cheered-on appalling animal cruelty, often linked to equally shocking mistreatment of human beings including criminals, slaves and Christians. Just focusing on animals, the emperor Titus (79–81AD) celebrated his imperial inauguration with the killing of 9000 animals in the arena, and the emperor Trajan (98–117AD) celebrated his victory over the Dacians with the slaughter of some 11,000 animals in games that lasted 120 days. The Romans pushed the zebra, elephant and rhinoceros to extinction in North Africa and the tiger to extinction in Mesopotamia.

This carried over into the Middle Ages when animal slaughter was a largely upper-class avocation. The medieval nobility was addicted to hunting and they drove many European species to extinction.[90] As well as hunting and forest clearing for agriculture, sheer pig-headedness by governments in insisting on the destruction of wild animals and birds, led to the loss of many species. For instance, in England Henry VIII in 1532 and Elizabeth I in 1566 passed laws – the 'Vermin Acts' – insisting that all animals listed as 'vermin', that is animals not deemed to be useful, or a nuisance, or undesirable, or unnecessary, were to be exterminated; a bounty was placed on each creature killed, leading to widespread slaughter.[91]

Hunting remained an upper class 'sport' into the twentieth century. In 1910, for example, Theodore Roosevelt, former-US President, spent almost a year on a hunting safari in East Africa and Sudan; he actually touted it as a 'conservation' mission! In that time, he and his son Kermit killed some 512 animals including seventeen lions, twenty-nine zebras, twenty-seven gazelles, nine black and white monkeys, eight hippopotami, four crocodiles and many other animals and birds. Among the animals killed were eleven elephants. Talking about killing an old bull elephant, Roosevelt said that 'the big beast stood like an uncouth statue … he seemed what he was, a monster surviving over from the world's past, from the days when the beasts of the prime ran riot in their strength, before man grew so cunning of brain and hand as to master them.'[92] There is something sick in human psychology that persuades people, particularly white men, that by killing large animals, they assert their superiority. In the end its about patriarchal power, human dominance and blood lust. While there are still those who will pay money to hunt wild animals, it is still hard to understand what drives this senseless killing, except anthropocentric alienation from the natural world and the sense of power that comes from the fact that it could be done. All the excuses that contemporary so-called gun-toting hunters use, like 'getting out into nature', or 'having quality family time', in the environment are simply specious nonsense. The only justifiable reason to kill animals in the wild is the elimination of introduced, feral pest animals that prey on native species.

But what happened in the past through hunting pales into insignificance in light of the contemporary catastrophic loss of biodiversity. The blunt fact is that populations of vertebrate species have, on average, declined by sixty per cent since 1970 according to a 2018 WWF report.[93] An example is the African elephant whose numbers declined by more than a third between 2007 and 2014 due to the loss of land to expanding human populations invading their territories with the resultant conflict between humans and animals, as well as the demands of the illegal ivory trade. WWF says that humans are asking more and more from nature. 'We need 1.5 Earths to regenerate the natural resources we currently use; we cut trees faster than they mature, harvest more fish than oceans replenish, and emit more carbon into the atmosphere than forests and oceans can absorb.'[94] Animal populations continue to decline with the loss of 58% of vertebrates, with freshwater species declining by an extraordinary 81% since 1970. Marine species have declined by 36% in that same period due to massive overexploitation for human consumption.[95]

Extinction, of course, is a natural process, but today we are involved in an extinction event that, according to International Union for Conservation of Nature (IUCN), is 'between 1000 and 10,000 times higher than the "background" or expected natural extinction rate.' In 2018 the number of threatened species was an extraordinary 16,928 plants and animals, but as the IUCN points out 'this may be a gross underestimate because less than 3% of the world's 1.9 million described species have been assessed by the IUCN Red List of Threatened Species'. There are an estimated thirteen to fourteen million species on earth. The key issues in the decimation of biodiversity are habitat loss, land degradation, over-exploitation (like over-fishing), pollution, disease, invasion of introduced feral species and global warming. But in the end, it all comes back to us. 'The number of threatened species is likely to increase rapidly in regions where human population growth rates are high.'[96]

A particularly bad example of species extinction is Australia, which has a unique flora and fauna. At present many of Australia's 975 reptile species are under threat. Feral and pet cats and foxes are the most destructive threat that these reptiles face, with about 650 million killed each year by cats.[97] Another threat to Australia's reptiles is the introduced cane toad. Native reptiles eat the toad, but have no resistance to its toxicity. Climate change is also linked to a massive increase in the frequency and intensity of bushfires in Australia since European settlement.[98] In the 2019–2020 bushfire season in Australia, it is certain that more than one *billion* native animals died.[99] These threats, linked to loss of habitat, place many Australian species under increasing threat.

Similarly, it is estimated that one third of all species across the US need some form of conservation action. These include butterflies, freshwater fish, grizzly bears, bats, turtles, birds and even the rusty patched bumble bee. Species are under pressure because of forest destruction, the draining of wetlands for industrial-scale agriculture, urbanization, the use of pesticides, hunting and above all climate change which is leading to shifts in weather patterns, rising temperatures and altered rainfall patterns, placing animals in danger that cannot adapt quickly.[100] These same extinction scenarios can be found across the world.

Any illusion that things are getting better was shattered with the May 6 2019 release of the UN-sponsored report from the Intergovernmental Science-Policy Platform on Biodiversity and Ecosystem Services (IPBES) panel. The report states unequivocally that species extinction due to habitat loss is already far higher than the average losses over the last ten million years. Extinction rates are set to rise, especially with the expansion of agriculture to feed ever-increasing human numbers. The report finds that around one million animal and plant species are now threatened with extinction, many within decades, more than ever before in human history. 'The average abundance of native species,' it says, 'in most major land-based habitats has fallen by at least 20%, mostly since 1900. More than 40% of amphibian species, almost 33% of reef-forming corals and more than a third of all marine mammals are threatened.' The extinction picture is less clear for insect species, but available evidence supports a tentative estimate of 10% being threatened.[101] Among animals, the Report says that the main extinction drivers are changes in land and sea use, direct exploitation of organisms, climate change, pollution and invasive alien and feral species.

While climate change is currently ranked third as an extinction cause, its impact is going to increase over the next decades, surpassing the impact of land clearing and marine over-exploitation. While most of the contemporary extinction scenarios are occurring in tropical countries, this doesn't excuse the appalling records of developed countries like the United States and Australia.

Half earth

Someone who has been talking about biodiversity loss for many years is the Harvard socio-biologist, Edward O. Wilson. He is especially concerned about the 'millions of kinds of fungi, algae and most diverse of all, the insects and other invertebrate animals' that are fast disappearing. These, he says, 'are the foundation of the living world … the little things that run the Earth'. The present extinction rate is 'at upward of a thousand times the rate that existed before the coming of humans'.[102] Wilson warns that world-wide today, largely as a result of human induced climate change, we are looking at almost 35% of all present species becoming extinct by 2050. Many of these will be species we know little or nothing about, like the millions of fungi, algae and especially insects. To deal with this level of extinction, Wilson has proposed the notion of 'half earth'. Given the massive loss of biodiverse species, which will increase, he says, over the next thirty years, we need to take radical and integrated steps commensurate with the size of the problem. Wilson calls for us to dedicate half the surface of the earth entirely to nature, half for them, half for us.

The half earth idea could be applied immediately in developed societies that have extensive territorial landmasses like Canada, the US and Australia. Wilson says that national parks are not the answer to species loss, because in landscape terms they are the size of postage stamps, often confined islands in the midst of human occupation. They lose species precisely because they are isolated and disconnected from the broader landscapes which most species need to flourish. Wilson says: 'Half Earth is the goal, but it's how we get there, and whether we can come up with a system of wild landscapes we can hang onto. I see a chain of uninterrupted corridors forming, with twists and turns, some of them opening-up to become wide enough to accommodate national biodiversity parks, a new kind of park that won't let species vanish.'[103]

Wilson proposes that nations set aside half their land surfaces as wild territory for nature and other species by withdrawing human activity from these areas. Sure, people will protest, especially those impacted, but he argues that without the biosphere, humanity is doomed. He admits the solution is radical, but then the problem we face is catastrophic and concerns the very future of biodiverse life on earth. Ideally, developed democratic countries with large land masses and the resources necessary to achieve a half-earth solution could show the way here and begin to create large-scale regions that are sizeable enough to give species space to move. Wilson agrees that climate change is important, but that land fragmentation, destruction of coral reefs (he calls them 'the rainforests of the sea'), pollution of water, land, air and above all, the introduction of invasive feral species, as far greater threats to life on earth.

Australia would be an excellent place for the creation of a half earth. It is one of the hottest and driest places on the planet. Much of it's agriculture is dependent entirely on irrigation at enormous costs to landscapes through salinity and to the continent's river systems, which are often damned and drained multiple times. Enormous pressure is also placed on ground water reserves. For example, eastern Australia's Murray and Darling Rivers, the only extensive river system on the continent, are already suffering disastrous stress through water withdrawals for irrigation during periods of drought, resulting in several massive native fish-kills occurring in the Darling River in 2018–2019. A major cause of water loss in the Darling are large irrigated cotton-growing farms, a water intensive crop that is totally inappropriate in such a dry landscape as Australia. Owned by large, often foreign-controlled corporations, the water withdrawals from the Darling system are utterly irresponsible and motivated solely by profit. While the country can already support and feed itself several times over without irrigation and the destruction of a whole river system, with the growing impact of global warming, water is in increasingly short supply in Australia.

Nevertheless, the continent is uniquely placed to adopt the half-earth principle and the Darling River which flows through the western section of New South Wales could be the centre of a whole region where all agricultural production ceased and the half-earth principle applied. At least sixty percent of the landscape is uninhabitable desert, or at best, marginal land. It would not require a lot of population disturbance to declare much of inner-Australia as a biodiversity sanctuary. All that is needed is conviction and the political will power. Other regions which Wilson suggests should be set aside for biodiversity, are the Amazon River basin, the Serengeti grasslands in north-western Tanzania near Lake Victoria, Siberia's Lake Baikal, the most ancient and deepest lake in the world, the Redwood forests of northern California, the Mallee scrubland of southern Western Australia and the McMurdo dry valleys of Antarctica. While some of these regions are already partly or entirely protected, the Amazon is again under serious threat in Brazil from slash and burn clearing and uncontrolled forestry.

What are we going to do with the people who live in the landscapes that will revert to nature? People today, especially in the developed world, are used to moving for work, learning new skills, or adjusting to new ways of living. Adaptability is what makes *Homo sapiens* so successful. People living in half-earth regions would be bought-out and assistance given to them to learn new skills, or support them if they retire. In developing countries money could be made available to improve urban living and provide the medical and family planning services to those who have moved into cities after leaving land that reverted to half-earth.

All of this is possible. It is just a matter of developing the will, the priorities and the policies to carry it out. That is why developed western countries should be the first to adopt the half-earth principle, because they have the environmental consciousness, expertise, wealth and ability to allow the principle to be realized.

To embrace Wilson's theory, we need a major shift in moral thinking and ethical reasoning, with a real commitment to the non-human world. Even those sympathetic to the half-earth thesis point out that the problem is that human self-interest, ignorance, greed and inertia are usually dominant and attempts to nationalise privately-owned land for the environment usually involve fierce fights, even in regions with a strong green consciousness. But while Wilson's proposal might not be realized totally, it points in the right direction and lays out the non-negotiable conditions for the survival of life on earth. Certainly, anyone who espouses the nature first moral principle will demand and work towards the realization of half-earth for biodiversity.

What can we do?

Half-earth is one effective way of preserving biodiversity. But what else can we do to fulfil the moral principle that nature and the earth come first?

First, the ethics governing artificial developments in the landscape like housing estates, marinas, golf courses and other developments that impact on, or destroy essential or important habitats such as wetlands for birds, or forests for animals with unique requirements like the koala, are easy to decide. The habitats come first because of the impact their destruction causes for biodiversity, for birds, animals, fish, or rare or endangered insects or plants. Given our present ignorance, we can never be certain how important the survival of insects or plants are in a specific area to the local fabric of life. These kinds of developments are usually found in developed countries where the ethical decisions are simple: the earth comes first. But the political and economic mechanics are often difficult and convoluted with pressure from vested interests.

However, big development projects, like dams for hydro-electricity, are nowadays often situated in developing countries. An example is the Mekong River which flows through China, Laos, Myanmar, Thailand, Cambodia and Vietnam with tens of millions of people dependent on it. Water levels have dropped dramatically recently, so that by mid-2020 the river in the Thai-Laotian border region was down some 8 meters below spill-over level. The reason is that China has built several large dams on the upper reaches of the Mekong to supply hydroelectricity with no concern for the needs of the river downstream, or the people dependent on it. But the Chinese are not alone. Laos has also built large dams, largely funded by Chinese money. China offers the specious excuse of flood mitigation, the same excuse it used when building the Three Gorges Dam on the Yangtze River. Another example of a massive intervention in an important river is the Grand Ethiopian Renaissance Dam along the Blue Nile which will have enormous downstream consequences, especially for Egypt 'by reducing arable land by up to 72% … causing what would be the largest water stress dispute in modern human history'.[104]

Such artificial interventions into the natural flow of large river systems, often promoted by engineers who can't see anything beyond their own discipline, cause massive damage to natural systems, as well as to the people dependent on those systems. While I accept that the stated aim is to help people by mitigating floods or providing hydro-electricity, I would argue that the basic moral principle that the preservation of particular landscapes and local biodiversity takes priority over human needs. Humans can adapt or find other solutions, especially if they are assisted; landscapes and biodiversity can't. Part of ethical decision-making, the part that is often lacking, is the application of the virtue of prudence, by which I mean a discerning wisdom, a circumspect care for the future, an ability to look at all the issues and see them in order of importance.

Another group of developments such as mining, oil exploration and other projects resulting in global warming can be easily dealt with ethically. Despite their demonstrated contribution to climate change, corporations and governments are still proposing opening-up new coal mines. We know burning coal leads directly to global warming which immediately outlaws it ethically; the notion of so-called 'clean coal' is complete nonsense. Often the specious justification put forward for developing these mines is that it gives the poor electricity, while no account is taken of the pollution that results.

Take, for example, India: while the country is still dependent on coal for seventy per cent of its power needs, the Indian government announced in February 2020 that it will no longer import coal, but rely on its own reserves. The use of coal is decreasing and the country is moving ahead quickly with the widespread installation of renewables through solar and wind. In ethical terms Western aid should be in the form of making every village self-sufficient by providing them with solar panels, wind turbines and batteries to store the power. Also, the notion that mining creates employment in developed countries is also specious because computer driven, autonomous machinery that needs only a minimum of human input is increasingly used in the industry. Only a tiny number of people are employed.

Once we get beyond developments that are only about profits for large corporations, we come to much more difficult ethical issues, especially where social justice and equity is involved. As a Catholic for whom social justice is important, I often find it difficult to balance human needs with the protection of the environment. Some, like Pope Francis, would argue that we need a double bottom line: care for humankind and care for the environment at the same time. I would agree that this should be the ideal, but I am unsure if we can always reach it. Certainly, it is not primarily the poor who are driving destructive climate change, nor chewing-up the world's resources. It is the fifteen per cent of people, including myself, who live in the developed world who produce more than half of the world's carbon emissions. As we saw, we are already chewing-up a planet and a half of earth's biocapacity each year. At the same time the developed world produces massive volumes of waste, including non-biodegradables like plastic. The world's biggest consumers of biocapacity are the Gulf states of Qatar, Kuwait and the United Arab Emirates, followed by the US, Australia, Canada and some of the European countries. So, before we start blaming developing countries and poor people for damaging the biosphere, we need to look at our own consumption and our massive environmental footprint. Equity demands that we acknowledge that it is not the poor who primarily threaten biocapacity, but the excesses of the rich.

Nevertheless, we cannot deny that the sheer weight of numbers of poor people also create serious problems for the environment and biodiversity. When people are starving and desperate, they understandably use the resources that are at hand without considering how destructive their behaviour might be, or what long-term impact it might have. For instance, people are often forced to use their diminishing forests and wood supplies for cooking and heating, as in Niger. Another horrendous practice is blast fishing where poor fishermen use dynamite or other explosives to stun or kill fish. In the process, they destroy the reefs housing the fish. An example is tuna fishing off Dar Es Salaam, Tanzania, where people use bombs that destroy entire coral reefs that are the breeding grounds for many other fish. This destructive form of fishing also happens in the seas off Lebanon, Malaysia, the Philippines, Indonesia and elsewhere. Also, with increasing population, especially in Africa, dispossessed people are pushing into regions and areas that were once the range of wild animals. Some African countries have tried to protect animals through a system of national parks, but unless these are effectively policed, it does little to protect the animals, especially from poaching. As humans crowd into animal ranges, this puts enormous pressure on animals, many are killed and this has led in large part to the loss of wild animal populations.

Human activity, how we feed, fuel, and finance our lives, is taking an unprecedented toll on wildlife and wild places. The top threats to species identified by the WWF link directly to human activities, including habitat loss and degradation and the excessive use of wildlife in overfishing and overhunting.[105] Many of the larger animals like the black and white rhino, are the most threatened. In Africa these animals are under serious threat from poaching because rhino horn is used in traditional Chinese and Asian medicine and sells for exorbitant prices. African forest and savannah elephants are also under threat because of the banned ivory trade, where China again is the largest market.

Overfishing is having an enormous impact on the world's oceans. Realization of this problem first came to light with the collapse of Canada's Newfoundland cod fishing industry in the early-1990s. The industry was destroyed by trawlers that within a decade simply fished out the whole of the Grand Banks. This same level of overfishing is now happening across the world as super trawlers and factory ships scour the oceans with vast demersal or bottom trawling nets that scoop-up massive numbers of fish. Already some 84% of the world's fish stocks are in danger of collapse. Governments need to strictly control and enforce limits on this kind of fishing.

In the light of these assaults on biodiversity it is hard to maintain the notion that so much human activity is rational when, in fact, it is utterly irrational with our economies posited on endless, infinite growth in a world of limited resources. Our failure to respond decisively to the overwhelming evidence of global warming and biodiversity loss is also utterly irrational, given the long-term disastrous consequences for us. The same applies to the continued mining of coal and fossil fuels, when we know that they are massive contributors to greenhouse gases. We continue to clear land and irrigate when we have known since the beginnings of agriculture that these practices will eventually lead to the destruction of the very landscape we're farming. In fact, the very notion that humans act rationally is essentially irrational because it assumes that our judgements are based on arriving at the best decision rooted in an objective assessment of all the information available. It presupposes the unlikely scenario that we are able to abstract from self-interest, greed, emotions, biases, social pressures and what religion calls 'sin'.

But before we confront the question what are we going to do, let us ask if there are any grounds for hope?

9

Are There any Grounds for Hope?

Dystopia and denial

It's easy to become very pessimistic when dealing with or discussing population. Comments like those of Frank Fenner and other distinguished scientists that *Homo sapiens* might well become extinct 'perhaps within a hundred years', can plunge us into depression, or cause us to withdraw from engagement with reality because their views are supported by such strong, plausible arguments. My comments about the irrationality of so much human behavior in the previous chapter doesn't help much either. This pessimism can be re-enforced by popular literature with a plethora of dystopic novels and movies coming out recently describing a terrible possible future world of environmental destruction and human displacement and misery.

Derived from the word 'utopia' from the title of Saint Thomas More's book *Utopia* (1516), the word describes an imaginary place where everything is socially perfect. 'Dystopia' describes the opposite: an imaginary place where everything is appalling and awful. Nowadays the word is often used to describe a post-global warming, or post-nuclear war, or post-pandemic world in which life has become virtually unlivable. Already there is evidence that a kind of eco-dystopia resulting from overpopulation worries people, especially those who are not in denial about global warming, biodiversity loss and environmental destruction. Concern centers on the kind of near-future world our children and grandchildren will inherit. Increasingly we are being infected by anxiety and a sense of powerlessness and despair in the face of these kinds of problems.

Over the last decade there has been no shortage of novelists and film-makers stepping-up to sketch out for us the dystopian, near-future world that threatens. Whether such novels and movies help or hinder our efforts to confront our problems remains to be seen, but they certainly focus our attention. One of the most well-known dystopian novels is Canadian Margaret Atwood's *The Handmaids Tale* (1985), now a multi-series TV drama. Set in New England in the near future, and depending on a few isolated verses from the Hebrew Scriptures, the totalitarian Republic of Gilead, the former United States, selects fertile women for powerful men to impregnate in a time when fertility is worryingly low because of environmental pollution. Atwood is also the author of *The Year of the Flood* (2009), which describes a future when there are only a few people left after a 'black plague' that sounds pretty much like swine flu. Another dystopia is sketched in Cormac McCarthy's *The Road* (2006) set in a devastated, post-apocalyptic US. Here a father and son travel through a destroyed landscape, struggling to survive. In a gender twist on *The Road*, mother and daughter love and survival in raw nature are described in Diane Cook's 2020 novel *The New Wilderness*. Here cities have become uninhabitable, especially for children, where pollution is so bad that childbirth is discouraged. The heroine and her sick daughter take refuge in the last remaining large wilderness, a kind of Wilson half earth, where the two become involved in an experiment to see if humans can exist in nature without destroying it.

Moving from North America to Britain in the 2019 novel *The Wall*, John Lancaster introduces us to a UK in a near-future period after 'the Change', when the effects of global warming are being realized as ice caps melt and the Gulf Stream no longer saves Europe from freezing. Ocean levels have risen and vast hordes of climate refugees swirl around the world looking for help. A desperately cold Britain has built a cement wall around itself to keep 'Others' out. The wall's young 'Defenders' bitterly resent the 'Olds' who have created this catastrophe by their failure to address the planet's ills and have, as *The Wall* puts it, 'irretrievably fucked-up the world'. No one wants to have children and it has become a form of national service to be a 'Breeder'. It is a frightening, dark, miserable existence.

While most readers treat these books as fiction, they create a pervading sense of looming disaster. In this context, people react in predictable ways: for some its denial, either outright or unconscious, others despair, or panic; and for a minority, a determination to act to change the threatening trajectory. It is this type of determination that fuels organizations like Extinction Rebellion and the Greta Thunberg-inspired school strikes across the developed world.

Given the ecological disaster facing us, it's understandable that we regress to denial. The human tendency to deny inconvenient realities is a normal reaction and we all do it. Our responses are not just individual, because we are very good at what sociologist Kari Norgaard calls 'socially organized denial', narratives that help us deflect the implications of threatening problems.[106] She quotes a young American university student saying: 'I have all this information, [but] what the hell do I do with it; I'm not sure one person can make [much] difference.' Norgaard says that there is pressure to avoid such issues altogether in social interactions. People may well be aware of the problems facing us and feel passionate about them, but there are social norms about how controversial and confronting you can get in social situations. There is real pressure not to make other people feel disturbed by mentioning threatening realities. As a result, we fit our emotions and comments into social norms that constrict what we say.

Underlying social denial is a kind of passive, exhausted, even fatalistic acceptance of disaster scenarios like record-breaking heat, increasing bouts of wild weather, or intense wildfires. COVID-19 is similar: it's all too much to take in, so we just accept it as the new normal and try to get on with life within the constraints the pandemic imposes. With threats like COVID-19, we deal with what we can't avoid, then try to turn off and pretend that things are normal, or that they'll change sometime soon.

But denial goes deeper. The American cultural anthropologist Ernest Becker argued that denial of inconvenient truths is fundamentally rooted in the realization that eventually every living thing will die. He says that to distract ourselves from the reality of death we have constructed complex religious, cultural and political defence systems to create meaning and purpose in life and thus to stave-off the inevitability of dying. The main thesis of Becker's influential 1973 book, *The Denial of Death* is that 'the idea of death, the fear of it, haunts the human animal like nothing else; it is a mainspring of human activity – activity largely designed to avoid the facticity of death, to overcome it by denying in some way that it is [our] final destiny.'[107] We construct immortality projects of one sort or another because the reality of death is too much to take-in.

To stave-off the vulnerability that death threatens, Sigmund Freud argues, we demand illusions, we give 'precedence [to] what is unreal over what is real'.[108] Drawing on Freud's analysis, Becker says that we indulge these illusions because 'the real world is simply too terrible to admit; it tells [us] that we are small, trembling animals who will decay and die. Illusion changes all this, makes us seem important, vital to the universe, immortal in some way.'[109] Becker argues that the rock-bottom motivation for human behaviour is our biological need to control and obfuscate the cause of our anxiety, our knowledge that eventually we will die. Both Freud and Becker were writing within the context of secularised Judaism and Becker died young at the age of 49 from colon cancer in 1974, just after he finished writing *The Denial of Death*. He argued that all of us engage in some type of heroic immortality project that involves us in something that will outlast us. We want to be part of something bigger, more long-lasting than ourselves, something eternal. Becker says that this is where religion comes in; it gives us a sense that we are living for something good that is beyond the self, something transcendent. In this context the greatest hero is the saint, the person who has transcended self and lived for God and others.

Here Becker gives us a clue as to why it is so difficult to get people to confront environmental destruction and overpopulation. Both these realities threaten the constructed rhythms of life and the certainties and immortality projects we have constructed and upon which we rely. We constantly struggle to maintain normality and, as Norgaard says, we collude with each other in doing this. Threats like global warming, environmental breakdown and overpopulation need to be kept at a safe distance. The more obvious they become, the more we dig in and look for ways to distract ourselves.

In this situation the first thing we have to do is to admit to ourselves the seriousness of the problems we face because nowadays there is increasingly nowhere to hide. Young people, like Greta Thunberg get it, but deluded, death-denying 'Olds', like conservative politicians, or global warming deniers, say that the students are 'immature', are being 'manipulated by activists'. They should stay in school until they 'grow-up'. Perhaps these self-important adults should reflect on Jesus comment that God hides the truth 'from the wise and intelligent and reveals it to little children' (Matthew 11:25). He also reminds the high priests and scribes that it is 'out of the mouths of infants and nursing babies' (Matthew 21:16) that wisdom will come.

Based on Becker's analysis of denial, psychologists have tried to develop mechanisms to deal with the kind of resistance that people throw-up against confronting hard issues like overpopulation, biodiversity loss and global warming. It is often difficult to get people discussing these issues, but when you get them talking, many demonstrate that they're well aware of what's happening and are concerned about it.

But everyone struggles with the sheer breadth and complexity of the issues and especially their powerlessness in the face of them. As a result, we revert to denial saying it's not urgent, or we cast those who talk about it as 'catastrophists' who exaggerate the problem, or we project the issue into a nebulous future which doesn't involve us. Even when acknowledged, the solutions that are proposed are tinkering with the system, or minor modifications. To survive we live in a dual reality: we know we're facing monumental problems, but we live as though we weren't. We turn the unthinkable into the normal and while we feel guilt for not acting, we need order and stability and want to protect ourselves from the chaos overpopulation and global warming threaten.

A Different kind of dystopia

A very different kind of dystopia is described by those who believe that the most important problem we face is not overpopulation, but the polar opposite, the decline in population numbers in the developed world. This is a sign of 'decadence', as in the title of *New York Times* columnist Ross Douthat's 2020 book, *The Decadent Society*.[110] By 'decadence' Douthat means the decay of Western civilization, particularly in the US. This is characterised by cultural decline, economic stagnation and intellectual exhaustion. One of the key causes of decadence, according to Douthat, is 'below-replacement fertility'. His argument is that as birth rates fall, average age increases and creativity disappears. According to Douthat, this leads to societies that are already into a kind of risk-averse, terminal decline that results in cultural and intellectual sclerosis. One is tempted to reply – perhaps unfairly – that in that case the most creative societies should be those with the highest reproduction rates like Niger, Nigeria, or Chad where populations are booming.

Here I am not arguing that the West is in good cultural shape. In fact, I believe it is in serious decline, as evidenced by post-modern individualism. But I think that the far more important challenge facing us is not a culturally decadent, sclerotic West, but the fact that with global warming and overpopulation, we are already moving from dystopic fiction to reality because the worst aspects of the climate crisis are already hitting us and we may soon hit a tipping point that takes us into an irreversible decline. In the end there is something myopic about Douthat's concerns. They are very first world, even very narrowly American.

The simple fact is that we are already feeling the effects of global warming with some of the hottest, driest years of drought on record in many parts of the world, with an increasing incidence of intense wildfire even as far afield as the tundra of Siberia. In addition to fires, we've had hurricanes and storms that wreak havoc; island nations like Kiribati and low-lying coasts have already begun the drowning process. Niger vividly illustrates the consequences of not acting. I have already outlined the landscape constraints which the Sahara Desert and the semi-arid Sahel region impose on Niger. But the key issue here is runaway population. Given the already degraded country's very limited resources, the population is already totally unsustainable, especially when hit by drought. This will lead to a life-and-death struggle for ever-decreasing basic resources like food and water. This is the real decadence. But Niger is a microcosm of Sub-Saharan Africa. We need to remind ourselves again of the population statistics. In 2020 the population of the continent was 1.3 billion. By 2050 it will be around 2.4 billion, a totally unsustainable number. Parallel population statistics apply across the world and while I agree that the cultural decline of the West is important, maintaining a livable world is even more important.

Gaia

Before we turn to the attitudes of the mainstream religions to population, I want to refer to a secular approach to the environment with religious overtones, the concept of Gaia. In a way, the Gaia hypothesis is an attempt by a scientist to develop a dynamic approach to the natural world. In Greek mythology the word 'Gaia' referred to the earth in general, or to a vaguely personal goddess living within the earth and governing it.

In the mid-1970s, the chemist and futurist, James Lovelock, 'adopted' Gaia. He posited the notion that the earth developed and continues to maintain a self-organizing, self-regulating system which we don't control and which sustains life and is itself alive. Gaia, the earth, is a living organism that will ultimately respond to the brutality and abuse that humanity inflicts upon it. For Lovelock the many different parts of nature only make sense in terms of the whole; humankind derives its meaning solely from earth and human needs and aspirations must be subsumed to those of earth. The Gaia concept led to a discussion of the ethical rights of nature and its self-regulating capacity to rid itself of disruptive elements, like human beings, as it seeks equilibrium.[111] Lovelock's Gaia concept has much in common with the notion of a sense of living presence in nature. Nature is a dynamic reality that transcends humankind and that draws together all of the separate living realities that go to make-up the web of life. It created us through evolution, gives us life and sustains us, but has an existence and dynamism of its own that is totally independent of us. We don't constitute its meaning or *raison d'être*. Nature is the primal form of existence that we all share, the life force underlying all that exists.

By 2007 Gaia had become a vengeful goddess in Lovelock's next book *The Revenge of Gaia*.[112] He predicted that we are on the edge of an apocalyptic dark age as a result of runaway 'global heating' which, he predicts, could occur as soon as the 2050s, which means that many young people alive now will be affected by it. Lovelock is unequivocal that the root problem is overpopulation and that the expansion of human numbers is what has disrupted the whole earth system. He paints a dystopian picture of the future, with the breakdown of central government leaving a bevy of struggling, starving humans in the last inhabitable places on earth, Antarctica and Greenland. He describes an earth out of balance and it's going to take 100,000 years to regain equilibrium. Whether humankind will survive is doubtful. The only way out, Lovelock says – and this is where I part company with him – is through an ultra-high-tech civilization, maintained by nuclear power.

But the notion of Gaia is a good introduction to a topic not high on Lovelock's list, the role of religion in questions surrounding overpopulation and how we deal with it.

10

The Role of Religion

Religion—part of the problem?

So, to return to the title of the previous chapter: are there any grounds for hope? Here I want to try to show that there are. We already know that facts, statistics and abstract arguments often lack persuasive power for most people. Intellectual presentations usually don't motivate us to take action, or change behavior. We have also lost the ability to deal with big picture issues because our ethical systems are preoccupied, even obsessed, with subjectivity, personal rights and the injustices, needs and hurts, real or imagined, of individuals, groups and minorities. We have lost focus on the bigger, all-embracing moral pictures that challenge us, so we lack an over-arching moral framework to deal with population. That is why I have tried to articulate a non-anthropocentric, fundamental principle that highlights biodiversity and the maintenance of the integrity of the earth before everything else, including the needs of humankind. But that too can remain abstract and impersonal. It seems divorced from real people and it doesn't tell you how to help the people of Kiribati in a practical way, let alone those in rural Niger. It gives you a principle that governs behaviour, but it doesn't give you a context to apply that to reality.

This is where faith and belief can enter the picture. Up until now religion has been absent from discussion of population, largely because none of the great faiths, including Christianity, have developed the sophisticated ethical apparatus necessary to assess the morality of population limitation, let alone offer any substantial moral guidance on the issue. As Thomas Berry says Christianity's greatest failure in its whole history is its failure to deal with the devastation of the planet. The result is that the discussion has been mainly carried on in scientific and factual terms by biologists, demographers and economists.

Understandably, many will be suspicious of religion, especially Catholicism and Islam, because believers often seem to be more part of the problem than its solution. Many people ask: 'What about the Catholic ban on contraception?' This objection is re-enforced by the fact that we've already seen that the church has done little to encourage family planning in developing countries like Kiribati. Another example is Kenya, a country with a serious population problem. There Catholic Archbishop Zacchaeus Okoth was reported in January 2018 renewing 'the war against contraceptives at a time when Kenya had won a global [family planning] award for accelerated use of birth control.' He complained that fertility rates in two provinces in western Kenya had declined due to the use of contraception, the very thing the family planning program had set out to do.[113]

Let me say that as a Catholic I accept that much of the criticism of institutional Catholicism's performance in the area of fertility and population is justified. Many bishops have been irresponsible, particularly Pope John Paul II in his obsession with the so-called 'contraceptive mentality' and the evils of contraception. This has been reflected by some bishops' conferences across the world, particularly in poorer, developing countries like Kenya, where Catholics are 33% of the population and the Philippines where Catholics constitute 80%.

However, I say this with an important caveat: when dealing with religions and churches, you always have to make a distinction between what religious leaders say and what people actually do. For instance, Catholics in countries like the United Kingdom, the US, Canada and Australia used to be accused of having lots of children, of 'breeding like rabbits'. However, both historical and contemporary evidence shows that this is a caricature. For example, Catholic fertility in Australia has always remained pretty much in lock-step with national fertility rates since the late-nineteenth century and is now slightly below that of the rest of the population.[114] But, many argue, that is not true of developing countries. However, the facts don't support that: in the Philippines the fertility rate in 1960 was 7.27 births per woman; in 2020 it was 2.58. In Kenya in 1960 it was 7.79; in 2020 it was 3.52. These drops occurred despite the opposition of Catholic bishops in both countries.[115]

Some historical perspective is useful here. It was really not until the late-nineteenth century when mechanical contraceptives became widely available that family planning began to be publicly discussed. It was only then that, as John T. Noonan says, 'a vigorous attack on birth control' came to the fore in Catholicism.[116] Prior to that Catholic discussion of reproduction was confined to moral theology. But from about the late-nineteenth century an emphasis began to be placed on fertility and sexual issues, especially by medical professionals, and there was widespread scientific concern about an imagined declining birth rate. It was largely in the wake of this concern that the churches denounced contraception as against the natural law and encouraged large families from the pulpit. However, all the evidence points to the fact that ordinary Catholics, particularly women, made up their own minds and priestly exhortations were only a small part of their decision-making. Economic survival and the needs of children already born were the most persuasive arguments for them. It was really only for a brief period after the Second World War that lay Catholics allowed the church into their bedrooms, but after the 1968 encyclical *Humanae vitae* condemning contraception, the large majority of Catholics rejected church teaching and made their own conscientious decisions about fertility. As we've seen nowadays it is European Catholic countries whose populations have dramatically dropped below ZPG.

But before looking at the role of religion in population policy, it is important to know the comparative numbers of the major world religions.[117]

> Christianity 2.38 billion = 31.2% of world population
> Islam 1.8 billion = 24.1%
> Unaffiliated 1.2 billion = 16%
> Hindu 1.1 billion = 15.1%
> Buddhist 0.5 billion = 6.9%
> Folk religion 0.4 billion = 5.7%
> Others 0.1 billion = 0.8%
> Jewish faith 0.1 billion = 0.2%

Thus, worldwide in 2015 there were 6.38 billion people with religious affiliations, with Islam the fastest growing religion. So, what role can religion play in population policy? Here I will focus on the major Abrahamic traditions.

First Judaism

There is no explicit biblical or rabbinical reflection on population as such, but there is much discussion of fertility in the Hebrew scriptures (the Old Testament), the Talmud (the body of Jewish law) and in the teachings of the rabbis. At the core of the Jewish theology of fertility is the biblical command to 'be fruitful and multiply and fill the earth' (Genesis 1:28). God later makes a covenant, or agreement, with Abraham: 'You shall be the ancestor of a multitude of nations … I will make you exceedingly fruitful' (Genesis 17:4-6). God extends that covenant promise to the entire Hebrew people: 'I will love you, bless you and multiply you; [I] will bless the fruit of your womb' (Deuteronomy 7:12). The Hebrew scriptures also have a tradition of God making barren women fertile. The best-known example is Sarah, Abraham's wife, who had her son Isaac when the couple were very old (Genesis 21:1-22).

Intimately linked to human fertility is the fertility of nature. Immediately following God's promise that He will multiply the Jewish people in the Book of Deuteronomy, there is a commitment to bless 'the fruit of your ground, your grain and your wine and your oil, the increase of your cattle and the issue of your flock' (Deuteronomy 7:13).

The Talmud also emphasizes the duty of having children. Rabbi Eliezer says: 'He who does not engage in the propagation of the race is as though he sheds blood; for it is said, "whoever sheds man's blood, by man shall his blood be shed," and this is immediately followed by the text, "And you, be you fruitful and multiply."'[118] The rabbis apply this teaching to the practicalities of procreation, one school claiming that a couple should have at least a son and a daughter, another school claiming there must be two sons, like Moses. More children are a blessing from God.

It is understandable that this theme of fertility would be prominent in contemporary Jewish thought after the horrendous losses that European Jewry suffered in the Holocaust. The American Jewish Committee reflected on this in a 2002 report on Jewish population. It showed that in the late-1990s the average population growth for world Jewry, except in Israel, was flat and even falling below replacement. The cause was the loss of many diaspora Jews through marriage to non-Jews with the children being brought-up outside Judaism. The figures are quite startling: 50% of US Jews and more than 30% of Canadian and Australian Jews marry out. In Russia and the Ukraine, the figure is about 70%, it is 50% in France and 40% in the UK. The American Jewish Committee concluded: 'Based on these facts, many Jews believe that one of the critical challenges today is the issue of Jewish survival in the diaspora.' They argue that 'the low Jewish birth rate, along with high rates of intermarriage and assimilation, pose a grave danger to the Jewish people's … survival.'[119] This has led American Rabbi David M. Feldman to argue that 'Jews have the paradoxical right to work for the cause of population control while regarding themselves as an exception to the rule.'[120] Among the Orthodox and Hassidic communities, there is a high fertility rate. They don't marry out and avoid assimilation into the wider community.

In Israel there has been an understandable emphasis on having children to replace those lost in the Holocaust and this is certainly reflected in Israel's population growth. The country has an exceptionally high fertility rate for a developed country: 2.97 children per woman in 2021, about the same as it was in 1995. Encouraged by government, the country's 2021 population was 8.78 million, a doubling since 1990. Most of this population increase comes from births rather than from immigration which now constitutes only 12% of the country's population growth.

Islam

Muslims are often accused of trying to out-breed other groups, especially where there are sizeable Muslim minorities, as in India, Myanmar, and Western Europe, where the claim is a reaction to the recent large influx of Muslims from Syria and Africa. While Islam often does have a high birth rate, in fact, the majority of the world's Muslims live in countries that have adopted quite effective family planning programs.

It is hard to generalise about Muslim attitudes to fertility because

Islam is a diverse faith and exists in many countries and cultures. However, except in extreme interpretations of religious law, Islam is not traditionally opposed to fertility control. As Cambridge Islamic scholar, Basim Musallam says: 'Muslims are free to control births … As long as compulsion is avoided, the provision of information, clinics, services, and devices can all be accommodated within the dominant interpretation of religious law without damage to its spirit.'[121] Several Muslim majority countries like Bangladesh, Iran and Indonesia have run successful family planning programs and have considerably reduced their population growth contradicting the prevailing narrative that Muslims are not interested in population limitation. However, the importance of marriage, family formation and procreation are central to Islam, although the Qu'ran recommends that births be spaced thirty months apart. However, there is opposition to fertility control among fundamentalists who see family planning as a way of limiting the Muslim birth-rate, a kind of Western 'genocide conspiracy'.

Iran is an interesting case of a country that has debated fertility control. In the late-1960s an inadequate and insensitive family planning program was initiated by the Shar's government. After the revolution of 1979 the Ayatollah Khomeini government was not per se opposed the use of contraception, but during the Iran-Iraq war (1981–1988) population size emerged as a propaganda tool, as well as a source of military muscle and soldiers for canon-fodder. Iran's population increased from 38.6 million in 1980 to 56.3 million in 1990, despite massive losses in the war. Fertility remained high (6.38 in 1980 and 5.62 in 1990), but after the war ended support for family planning, the wide availability of primary health care including contraception advice before marriage, programs promoting rural development and literacy, improvement in the status of women, delay in childbearing by younger couples, and wider time spans between births, have all helped to bring Iran's fertility rate down. Recently, more conservative governments haven't favored family planning and the fertility rate has risen from 1.82 in 2010 to 1.96 in 2020. However, this is a massive drop from 6.91 children per women in 1960. In 2021 the total population was 85.1 million

Indonesia, the country with the world's largest Muslim population (276.4 million in 2021), has not been as successful in controlling fertility as Iran, but for a developing, scattered island nation, it has achieved much. In 1960 the Indonesian fertility rate was 5.67; in 2021 it was 2.32. Another example is Muslim Bangladesh which cut its fertility rate through a successful family-planning program based on trained and literate village women going door-to-door dispensing contraceptives and explaining birth control to women, supported by a government-sponsored education program that prioritized girls. In contrast, Islamic Pakistan, like India, took a single-pronged approach, promoting IUDs in the 1960s. It paid doctors to insert them and women for having them inserted, leading to widespread corruption. Nevertheless, Pakistan's fertility rate fell from 6.6 in 1960 to 3.55 in 2021.

Despite these successes, the world Islamic population is growing, but the geographical spread is uneven, with the biggest increases occurring in Sub-Saharan Africa. Here, as we've seen in West Africa, the problem is not so much religion as the social and economic oppression of girls and women and the widespread denial of educational and job opportunities to them. Recent work by the Pew Research Center shows that 'Muslims will grow more than twice as fast as the overall world population between 2015 and 2060 and, in the second half of this century, will likely surpass Christians as the world's largest religious group.' Muslim numbers are expected to grow from 1.8 billion in 2015 to almost three billion in 2060. Most of this growth will be in Africa and the Middle East where Muslims have a median age of twenty-four. According to Pew, 'The main reasons for Islam's growth ultimately involves simple demographics. To begin with, Muslims have more children than members of the seven other major religious groups analyzed in the study. Muslim women have an average of 2.9 children, significantly above the next-highest group (Christians at 2.6) and the average of all non-Muslims (2.2). In all major regions where there is a sizable Muslim population, Muslim fertility exceeds non-Muslim fertility.'[122] In many Muslim countries, especially in where fundamentalist groups like Islamic State, Boko Haram, or Salafism are influential, family planning is seen as a Western plot to reduce the Muslim fertility and population numbers. Thus, it is as difficult for many Muslims as it is for some literalist-fundamentalist Christians, to take the population question seriously.

116

Christianity: Protestantism and Orthodoxy

Before looking at Christian views on fertility and population, I want to mention historian Lyn White's brief, but widely discussed 1967 article which argued that 'Christianity is the most anthropocentric religion the world has [ever] seen'. He argued that Christian theology saw nature as created exclusively to serve humankind, the only true image of God. He says that the biblical assumption is that we have a right to 'subdue and use' creation, and that nothing will change in human-nature relationships 'until we reject the Christian axiom that nature has no reason for existence save to serve man'.[123] White's article caused widespread controversy and is often quoted. In one sense, I agree with him; in another sense, his is profoundly wrong, as I hope the following discussion will demonstrate.

Turning first to the Protestant churches: the word 'Protestant' spans a wide spectrum of opinion on theological and ethical issues from liberal to conservative. There is a sense in which the World Council of Churches gives expression to views that are widely held across the more liberal Protestant spectrum, but it's still difficult to generalize about Protestantism on an issue like overpopulation. Part of the reason for this is that the first Protestants, Martin Luther and John Calvin, strongly emphasized the importance of individual salvation and each person's right to respond to a free relationship with God. Because of this notion of personal autonomy, the Protestant tradition is respectful of each individual's right not only to interpret scripture, but also to make conscientious individual moral decisions before God. While Evangelical (bible focused) Protestantism still tends to be very conservative on sexual and reproduction issues, approval of contraception has nowadays become normative throughout Protestantism. Nevertheless, Evangelicals are very active in enforcing what they see as Christian principles on issues like abortion through state legislation.

European Protestantism prior to the 1950s was supportive of family planning. 'There is agreement today among all serious Christian moralists,' influential Swiss theologian Karl Barth said, 'that ... generation and conception ... must always be a matter of free consideration and decision' by individual Christians.[124] He thought that the text 'be fruitful and multiply and fill the earth' (Genesis 1:28) no longer applied, because overpopulation was not good for the world and humankind. In a similar fashion, the German theologian, Dietrich Bonhoeffer, who was murdered by the Nazis in April 1945, was deeply concerned about population increase, although he opposed abortion. After World War II Protestant theologians like Reinhold Niebuhr, Paul Tillich and Jacques Ellul began looking at the whole question of marriage, reproduction and population pressures and there was a growing consciousness that the church had to move away from a purely reproductive view of marriage, to the promotion of the mutual love of the spouses as equal to, or more important than having children. This was also the period in which the contraceptive pill became widely available, and for the first time in history conception became controllable by individual women and married people. However, the focus was on the couple, mutual love and the morally justifiable use of contraception. It had little to do with a rapidly escalating world population. With the publication of *The Population Bomb* and the Neo-Malthusian emphasis on overpopulation and depopulation, a consciousness began to develop in more liberal Protestant circles of the need to respond to this.

In the decades after the 1960s the social justice movement come to prominence in both Catholic and Protestant circles. While not totally unsympathetic to population concerns, the notion gradually gained ground among many social justice-oriented Christians that secular neo-Malthusians like Paul Ehrlich and others were missing the point with their emphasis on too many people. According to social justice advocates, the central issue was not population, but poverty, lack of equity in the distribution of world resources and inequality between the rich world and developing countries. As a result, social justice advocates felt that the focus should be on Western nations assisting developing countries by generous aid, rather than on worrying about population numbers.

The Neo-Malthusians didn't help by their overt antagonism toward religion. In response from the mid-1980s suspicion grew among Christians that the Neo-Malthusians were largely motivated by an unconscious, or even conscious eugenic motivation. This is completely unfair because those concerned about population were not aiming at selective breeding by eliminating the 'unfit', but wanted to reduce population numbers through family planning. Nevertheless, many Christians felt that the burden of reducing population was falling almost exclusively on poor countries. Also, there was considerable suspicion of government-inspired coercion to limit population. This was deepened by the sterilization policies of successive Indian governments and the one-child policy in China. While mainstream Protestants believe that an individual can voluntarily seek sterilization, this should never be imposed, as it was in India with the financial support of Western organizations committed to population reduction. This rupture between Christian social justice advocates and secular Neo-Malthusians has never been healed.

If anything, this rupture has been deepened by US Evangelicals. Evangelicals have been influential throughout American history and this continues today. It is hard to get exact numbers, but there are probably some 40 to 75 million Evangelicals in the US. The main groups are the Southern Baptist Convention, the National Baptist Convention, the Assemblies of God, and various Pentecostal churches. They tend to be highly critical of mainstream Protestants whom they consider too liberal, especially on gender, family and sexuality. Above all, for Evangelicals, abortion has become *the* touchstone issue. Politically, they played important roles in the elections of George W. Bush and Donald Trump. In the Ronald Reagan years, they pressurized the administration to withdraw funding from International Planned Parenthood (IPPF) and other population initiatives. Their aim is to re-criminalize abortion and they continue to maintain significant political and judicial power.

Turning now to the Eastern Orthodox churches which, alongside Catholicism, are the most ancient of the Christian churches with a tradition reaching back to the apostles. Like the other churches in the first half of the twentieth century, Orthodoxy placed population concerns in the context of family ethics and the condemnation of birth control. The broader social context was the fear of Orthodox countries like Greece, Serbia, Bulgaria, Romania and Orthodox minorities in Albania and Turkey, that their populations were declining.

But a shift in attitude occurred around 1970 when the Orthodox emphasis shifted from reproduction to the mutual fulfillment of the spouses in marital love. As a result, these churches eased their stance against contraception. The Greek-American theologian, Nicon D. Patrinacos, representing progressive Orthodox believers, went further, unequivocally recognizing the reality of the population problem. He said that 'unlimited reproduction of our own kind has reached the point of impoverishing rather than enriching humanity ... Birth control is, in more than half of today's world, as important and as urgent as feeding the millions of starving. More births would mean more hunger, more pain, more deaths.'[125]

The world's leading Orthodox bishop, the Ecumenical Patriarch of Constantinople, Bartholomew I, has shown outstanding leadership on environmental issues and has been promoting ecological theology for many years. He sees ecology not only as a 'spiritual responsibility', but as a moral imperative. 'To commit a crime against the natural world is a sin. For human beings to cause species to become extinct and to destroy the biological diversity of God's creation; for human beings to degrade the integrity of the earth by causing changes in its climate, by stripping the earth of its natural forests, or by destroying its wetlands; for human beings to injure other human beings with disease by contaminating the earth's waters, its land, its air, and its life, with poisonous substances — all of these are sins.'[126] For Bartholomew ecology is not just a scientific issue; it is spiritual, moral and theological. The writer who most truly expresses Bartholomew's ecological theology is the Australian-American theologian, John Chryssavgis, who points to the essence of the crisis we face. 'We tend to call this crisis an "ecological" crisis ... [But] the crisis is not first of all ecological. It is a crisis concerning the way we perceive reality, the way we imagine or image our world.' He says that we objectify the world, treat it as 'god-forsaken'. We have to discover, he says, an 'alternative way of seeing ourselves in relation to the natural world'.[127] Chryssavgis is exactly right; we need an entirely new way of viewing the world.

Catholicism

Of all the Christian churches, the Catholic church comes in for most criticism from people concerned about population issues. Part of the reason is that it is, by far, the largest Christian community with 1.328

billion adherents in 2020.[128] Another cause is that much of Catholicism's growth is in developing countries where, at least at the level of bishops, it forbids contraception. However, at the grass roots level in these countries, it is often the church that provides most of the health care and education services that help lift people from poverty, and at that level, ordinary Catholics are far less strident about contraception.

Back in the 1960s during the Second Vatican Council, there were bishops who were aware of the population problem. As with many hot-button issues at the council, it was the Belgian Cardinal, Léon-Joseph Suenens, archbishop of Mechelen-Brussels, who highlighted the population question. Speaking on 29 October 1964 in the debate on the document *Gaudium et Spes* ('Church in the Modern World'), Suenens reminded the bishops of 'the immense problem arising from the population explosion and overpopulation in many parts of the world. For the first time we must proceed [to] … study [it] in the light of faith. It is difficult, but the world, whether consciously or not, waits for the Church to express her thought.' He was immediately supported by the then-87-year-old Lebanese-born Melkite Patriarch, Maximos IV Saigh, who said that 'demographic pressures in certain countries of particularly heavy population prevent any increase in the standard of living and condemn hundreds of millions of human beings to unworthy and hopeless misery. The council must find a practical solution. This is a pastoral duty.'[129] However, Suenens notwithstanding, the world is still waiting 'for the Church to express her thought' on population. Official Catholicism has said virtually nothing on the question, and what it has said is ill-informed. The problem is that the church's approach has been completely distorted by questions around the papal teaching against contraception.

This was highlighted when the contraceptive pill first came on the market in the 1960s. A key person in the development of the pill was Dr John Rock of Harvard Medical School, a practising Catholic, who was concerned about the need for world population control. For the first time in history an accessible and reliable contraceptive gave women freedom from the biological consequences of intercourse. There was much debate about the use of the pill in Catholic circles which came to a head in July 1968 with the publication of Pope Paul VI's encyclical *Humanae Vitae* in which he condemned all forms of artificial contraception, including the pill. This led to a major split within Catholicism, with many Catholics and priests abandoning the church. The question of population has subsequently been lost in endless debates about the morality of the pill. As ethicist, J. Bryan Hehir, puts it, 'The detailed discussion of contraception in Catholic moral theology has at times conveyed the impression that this one issue constituted the whole Catholic position on population ethics.'[130]

Sure, there have been passing references in official documents to population. In his 1967 encyclical *Populorum Progressio* ('The Progress of Peoples') Paul VI admitted that 'It is true that too frequently ... the size of the population increases more rapidly than the available resources ... From that moment the temptation is great to check the demographic increase by means of radical measures.' By 'radical measures' he meant contraception, sterilization and abortion. He admits that 'public authorities can intervene [in population growth], within the limits of their competence, by favouring the availability of appropriate information and by adopting suitable measures, provided that these are in conformity with the moral law and that they respect the rightful freedom of married couples.'[131] So having admitted that there is a role for public intervention, he retreats to the couple's decision regarding family size, thereby making fertility a largely personal decision.

His successor, John Paul II (1978–2005), unlike popes before him, often candidly discussed sex, marriage, gender and the body; many were surprized and some scandalized that a pope was so forthcoming on these issues.[132] However, John Paul had little sympathy for overpopulation. In his November 1981 letter on the family, he was critical of 'a certain panic deriving from the studies of ecologists and futurologists on population growth, which sometimes exaggerate the danger of demographic increase to the quality of life'. This led him to denounce 'as a grave offense against human dignity and justice' government intervention limiting couples' decision-making regarding children. 'Any violence,' he says, 'applied by such authorities in favor of contraception or, still worse, of sterilization and procured abortion, must be altogether condemned and forcefully rejected.'[133]

In his 1987 encyclical *Solicitudo Rei Socialis*, John Paul grudgingly admits that there is a population problem 'especially in the southern hemisphere'. But, side-stepping that, he immediately turns to the northern hemisphere where, he says, 'the nature of this problem is reversed: here the cause for concern *is the drop in the birth rate* [italics in original], with [an] aging ... population, unable to renew itself biologically.' He repeats his alarm at 'systematic campaigns against birth' which he describes as 'a tendency toward a form of racism, or the promotion of certain equally racist forms of eugenics'.[134] Just how a drop in the birth rate is a form of 'racism', let alone 'eugenics' makes absolutely no sense, but it probably springs from his relentless and emotional opposition to contraception. This opposition was rooted in his peculiar understanding of the human person. He argues that sexual intercourse is only truly human and moral within the strict context of monogamous marriage. In any other setting sexual intercourse is 'using' another person. He says that contraception degrades women by making them sexual objects. In a feminist and post-Freudian world this is incomprehensible, which perhaps explains his opposition to feminism which he saw as a Western liberal conspiracy to promote contraception and abortion.

But John Paul's involvement with the population issue was not just theoretical. He was also particularly active in the lead-up to the UN Population Conference in Cairo in September 1994 when 'for the first time in modern history [he] pitted the Vatican against most of the international community' and especially against the Clinton administration.[135] The previous Reagan administration had promoted a 'pro-life' policy and cancelled American contributions to the UN Fund for Population Activities, the IPPF and other family planning organizations. Reagan was responding to political pressure from Evangelicals and the anti-abortion lobby, as well as placating John Paul and promoting a strategic compact with the Vatican against the Soviet Union. When Bill Clinton became president in 1992, he restored federal funding for abortion and supported family planning through US-funded foreign aid programs. The battle lines with John Paul were drawn.

In the lead-up to the Cairo Conference the whole discussion of population had moved on from *control* of birth rates by whatever means, especially in developing countries, to a more co-operative approach that involved helping couples and particularly women in deciding their own fertility within the context of their particular circumstances. This was linked to an emphasis on broadscale health care for women and girls. But the problem that emerged prior to the Conference was that IPPF and Family Planning International, with support from the Clinton administration, were determined to include the declaration of the right to a safe abortion in the Conference document. This provoked John Paul. He was utterly determined to prevent the UN and the international community adopting a policy document that would legitimize contraception, access to safe abortion and to what was called 'reproductive health,' which in the pope's mind implied the right to an abortion. There was also concern among Vatican clerics about the influence of 'American feminism'. John Paul was determined to make a stand because he believed that he was called by God to save the world and civilization from the consequences of what he called the 'contraceptive mentality' which he equated with a 'civilization of death'. In his 'Letter to Families' (February 1994) he characterizes attacks on the family and the use of abortion and contraception as a symptom of a self-destructing civilization. 'We are facing,' he said, 'an immense threat to life: not only to the life of individuals, but also to that of civilization itself … civilization has become, in some areas, a "civilization of death".'[136] There was something hysterical about it all.

But it was in John Paul's encounter with the Secretary-General of the Population Conference, the Pakistani gynaecologist, Dr. Nafis Sadik, in a one-on-one encounter on 18 March 1994, that the pope's fury exploded. Based on her notes, Sadik recalls an angry pope who was convinced that the Clinton administration and Western feminists were using the conference to claim that contraception and abortion were inherent human rights and that they were using the cover of reproductive health and population as a way of imposing birth control and contraception on the developing world. According to Sadik, the pope said that 'Family planning can be practised only in accordance with moral, spiritual and natural laws', largely as defined by the papacy.[137] Given his idealized notion of women, he seemed blissfully unaware of the kinds of problems real women faced, especially in the developing world, from drunken or violent husbands, the fear of abandonment in poverty with several children, let alone the danger of rape. To experienced women doctors like Sadik, the pope lived in an unreal world of moral absolutes, totally divorced from reality. The day after his meeting with Sadik, John Paul issued a letter addressed to her, but really directed to world leaders, strongly proclaiming the anti-abortion and anti-contraception line claiming that 'population policy is only one part of an over-all development strategy'. He claimed that 'the very future of humanity' was at stake.[138] He phoned Clinton personally and used the papal diplomatic corps to pressure governments across the world.

The expectation that the Vatican would be supported by Muslim countries to subvert the Conference was only partially realized. The moderate Muslim view was expressed on the first day of the Conference by Prime Minister Benazir Bhutto of Pakistan who said that her country needed to 'check its rapid population growth' and added: 'It is not the future of the people of Pakistan to live in squalor and poverty … hunger and horror.' At the same time, she emphasized that Islam rejected abortion as a method of population control and she was supportive of the traditional family. Her views represented mainstream Islam and she clearly rejected the extreme views of Islamic fundamentalists. In the end the Vatican had to fall back for support on smaller Catholic countries like Malta, Ecuador, Honduras and Guatemala.

What did the Vatican achieve at Cairo? According to the US-based *National Catholic Reporter* very little. 'Rome may well have damaged itself as a moral force on the world scene and prevented itself from reaching a wider audience beyond the rock-hard conservatives who eagerly endorsed its ways.'[139] John Paul II was entirely to blame for this over-reach. He seemed to lack any understanding of the reality in which many Catholics and other people lived, especially in the developing world. He was besotted by his own narrow ideology that appeared to lack any pastoral or humane concern for real people. Regarding overpopulation, he had no suggestion whatsoever to offer as to how this might be confronted, except to say that it couldn't be through abortion, sterilization, or any program of sexual education that included contraception. His 26 year-long papacy was a disaster for serious Catholic consideration of the problem of overpopulation.

Even at the best of times Catholic moralists think of population within too narrow a context. What is lacking is reference to a comprehensive moral picture that transcends anthropocentrism. Nevertheless, Catholic ethicists like to claim that the church has maintained the link between population and other moral issues. J. Bryan Hehir says that 'The population problem [is] one strand of a larger fabric … While acknowledging the existence of a population problem, the [Catholic] view asserts that it is morally wrong and practically ineffective to isolate population as a single factor, seeking to reduce population growth without simultaneously making those political and economic changes which will achieve a more equitable distribution of wealth and resources within nations and among nations.'[140]

However, there's a problem here. The fact is that for all the discussion of justice and equity, important as they are, Catholic ethicists never actually get to the question of population. What happens is that conservative Catholics like John Paul II become stymied by the issues of abortion and contraception, and those of a more progressive bent by their preoccupation with social justice and an equitable distribution of wealth and resources. Certainly, there is genuine and increasing sympathy for environmental questions in Catholicism. Many recognize that ecology is important, but Lyn White is right to the extent that a pervasive anthropocentrism still dominates the whole Christian and especially the Catholic agenda and for most believers, humankind rather than the created world remains the primary image of God. The natural world runs a poor second and population falls off the agenda entirely.

For those of us who see depopulation as the central issue, the reality is that the more humans there are, the worse issues like climate change and biodiversity loss are going to be. It is true that there are dreadful inequalities in international distributive justice. Nevertheless, as the number of human beings continues to grow enormous pressure is put on the environment, more greenhouse gases are produced, whole ecological systems are destroyed and other species continue their slide into extinction. There are clearly profound, broad-scale ethical issues embedded in these destruction scenarios, but the anthropocentrism of most religious-ethical systems prevents people of faith bringing their power of moral reflection and persuasion to bear on the problem of ecological destruction, species extinction and loss of biodiversity. In other words, the whole approach to the population question remains trapped in the realm of the human. Christians generally, and Catholics particularly seem unable to grasp the fact that the pressing needs of nature might override personal reproductive rights, or papal teaching about such issues. But then along came Pope Francis.

Pope Francis and Laudato si'[141]

When in February 2013 Benedict XVI resigned as pope and the archbishop of Buenos Aires, Jorge Mario Bergoglio, was elected as Pope Francis, no one expected that global warming, the environment and the preservation of biodiversity would be become a dominant theme of his papacy. But that is precisely what has happened as care for 'our common home' has become a leading motif of the Bergoglio papacy.

Francis had been pope for two years when in May 2015 he penned perhaps the most radical and important papal encyclical ever issued, *Laudato si', mi' Signore* ('Praise be to you, my Lord') [LS], addressed to 'every living person on this planet' about 'care for our common home'. The encyclical is a challenging and critical reflection on the whole structure of life and culture in the contemporary world, in the process confronting some deeply held, but destructive Christian traditions. LS moves theology away from the notion that we are stewards of the earth to use as we decide, because we alone are made in the image and likeness of God, to an all-embracing sense of our biological embeddedness in the earth and our intimate connection with it. In a post-modern age of fragmented thought, Francis takes an integrated approach that essentially calls us to a kind of cultural revolution. More important than Francis' repudiation of much of the politics, economics, technology, capitalist theory and denialist rhetoric of the post-modern world, is the theological and philosophical revolution that he points towards. He radically questions anthropocentric human dominance over nature and he reintegrates humankind back into the biological matrix from which we emerged by emphasising the connectedness of all reality. He says that it is above all the mystics who 'experience the intimate connection between God and all beings', something, he says, that we desperately need to recover. He continues: 'Rather than a

127

problem to be solved, the world is a joyful mystery to be contemplated with gladness and praise.'

But his mysticism is grounded in reality because LS gives no comfort to global warming deniers, technologies 'based on the use of highly polluting fossil fuels, especially coal', environmental wreckers who strip the earth of natural forests, or destroy wetlands, or those who have 'blind confidence in technical solutions'. Francis is critical of thinking 'of different species merely as potential "resources" to be exploited, while overlooking the fact that they have value in themselves', and he points out that we are biologically intimately connected to the world because 'a good part of our genetic code is shared by many living things'. Nature, he says, 'cannot be regarded as something separate from ourselves, or as a mere setting in which we live. We are part of nature.' *We are part of nature*: this is a message that runs through LS as Francis radically re-situates and re-roots humankind in the natural world.

The deepest shift that LS proposes is theological as he transposes the tradition's emphasis from anthropocentrism to a focus on the primacy of the earth and nature, in the process challenging the whole Catholic and Christian tradition to rethink the relationship between humankind and the earth. LS overthrows some 1750 years of tradition by side-stepping the notion of the human person as a body/spirit composite, a notion that entered Christian theology via the third-century Neo-Platonist philosophers and later through Saint Augustine (354–430) and other early theologians. Francis jettisons this paradigm and re-roots the theological tradition in scripture, specifically in Genesis: 'The creation accounts in the book of Genesis contain, in their own symbolic and narrative language, profound teachings about human existence and its historical reality. They suggest that human life is grounded in three fundamental and closely intertwined relationships: with God, with our neighbour and with the earth itself.' In other words, our relationship with the natural world is restored and Francis sees it as just as important as our relationship with God and with others. He also says that 'the Bible has no place for a tyrannical anthropocentrism unconcerned for other creatures'. The word 'anthropocentrism' crops-up regularly in a negative context in LS: he talks of 'distorted anthropocentrism', 'excessive anthropocentrism', and 'misguided anthropocentrism'. He re-enforces this by saying that 'nowadays, we must forcefully reject the notion that our being created in God's image and given dominion over the earth justifies absolute domination over other creatures … [Rather] this implies a relationship of mutual responsibility between human beings and nature.' This is a profound shift because Francis has undermined the whole anthropocentric paradigm.

Throughout most of its history Christianity denigrated the body and matter; materiality was seen as antithetical to spiritual growth and the search for God. Since the Neo-Platonists and Augustine introduced the body/soul dualism and the Platonic notion of the hierarchy of being into Christianity, church theology has been besotted with the absolute priority of the human. The notion of hierarchy of being was an arrangement in which God was supreme and every other reality was arranged according to their importance (God, angels, humans, animals, plants, matter, nothingness) with humankind just below the angels and above everything else. This was re-enforced by the medieval introduction of the concept of natural law, which significantly is nowhere mentioned in the encyclical, but which gave priority to human reason. In the tradition derived from these sources everything in the world plays second fiddle to humankind and its needs. No matter what their rhetoric about environmentalism, the churches have been crippled by this kind of anthropocentric theology that has dominated their unconscious reactions and guided their value judgments. The encyclical finally liberates Catholicism from this.

In one extraordinary step Francis takes us beyond the dominant anthropocentric paradigm and restores a genuine sense of what Thomas Berry, following Pierre Teilhard de Chardin (who is mentioned in LS), has called our 'biological connectedness' with the whole cosmos. By this Berry means that life is an interactive continuum from the most primitive forms to the most highly evolved and complex. We are not separate creatures whose lives and value somehow stand outside the rest of creation. We are a constituent part of nature because all life is profoundly related genetically. It is the genes that pass on the ever-increasing complexity of life. The realization of our genetic connectedness with everything else means that, unless we are prepared to destroy something of ourselves, we must work to preserve our common life.

This immediately places us in a humbler perspective; we are not separate and over and against the world, but an intimate part of it. The world is bigger than us and we must take it seriously and recognize its autonomy. 'It would also be mistaken,' Francis says, 'to view other living beings as mere objects subjected to arbitrary human domination. When nature is viewed solely as a source of profit and gain, this has serious consequences for society … The ultimate purpose of other creatures is not to be found in us.'

Francis is also critical of short-term politics and is openly contemptuous of the lack of vision of the world's leadership cadre. Politicians, he says, are besotted with 'the mindset of short-term gain'. Francis challenges them to show 'a testimony of selfless responsibility'. What is needed, he says, is 'a healthy politics … capable of reforming and coordinating institutions, promoting best practices and overcoming … bureaucratic inertia'. Columnist Ross Douthat has critically, but correctly understood that the encyclical is far more than just an attack on climate change deniers. It is a critique of 'the whole "technological paradigm" of our civilization, of all the ways (economic and cultural) that we live now'.[142] That's close to the mark, because Francis is clearly saying that we cannot continue along the trajectory on which we are now headed, because it will lead to environmental and human catastrophe.

But on the specific topic of population, Francis focuses solely on social justice stances. Speaking about global inequality, he says that some people narrow our environmental problems to 'a reduction in the birth-rate … To blame population growth instead of extreme consumerism … is one way of refusing to face the issues.' That's patently wrong, given that those concerned about overpopulation also strongly support a lowering of consumerist living standards. He is critical of 'certain policies of "reproductive health"' and claims that 'demographic growth is fully compatible with an integral and shared development'. However, he then seems to moderate his claim by saying that 'attention needs to be paid to imbalances in population density, on both national and global levels' and he seemingly acknowledges that 'a rise in consumption' in developing countries, would actually result in environmental pollution and waste treatment problems, as well as 'loss of resources and quality of life'. However, the dismissive reference to 'reproductive health', casting it as a kind of UN-inspired, Western plot to stop the poor having children is particularly unfortunate, because it is precisely at the local level where religion plays an important educational role. In many developing countries churches provide a supportive and caring community where reproductive information can be made available and where women and couples can discuss moral issues with informed people. Both women and men can be helped to understand that high fertility is not 'natural', let alone the will of God. This needs to be accompanied by practical medical help, including contraceptive advice.

Underlying his criticism of reproductive health is Francis' failure to recognize the contribution of women. This is the one glaring omission in an otherwise impressive papacy. While he has talked condescendingly about the so-called 'feminine genius', he has done nothing structural about acknowledging women's absolute equality as human beings and as baptised members of the church. Catholicism lags behind the secular world and key international bodies in affirming women's contributions to society, culture and to human betterment. This is a major blind spot for Francis.

Francis also says in LS that 'anthropocentrism need not necessarily yield to "biocentrism", for that would entail adding yet another imbalance, failing to resolve present problems and adding new ones'. I'm not so sure of that. There will always be tension between humans and the environment, especially when we become greedy, or when there are too many of us. So, to protect the natural world I would argue that *the* primary ethical principle has to be biocentric, that is the earth comes first; without it, we will be homeless. As Francis says, the natural world is not derived from us and, I would add, transcends us. As a result, we have to move beyond an anthropocentric to a biocentric ethic. Francis tries hard to keep ecology and social justice together, but I'm not sure if he succeeds. That's because I don't think you can, much as I would like to think otherwise. The primary moral emphasis has to be on the earth; the natural world comes first.

While Francis is profoundly critical of anthropocentrism, he never *really* embraces a theology and morality based on biocentrism and the centrality of the earth. That's probably understandable given his background. For a Catholic, let alone a pope, Francis has brought the church far beyond everything on environmental issues that has gone before. But Catholicism does need to take that final step beyond anthropocentrism and embrace as its primary moral principle the wonderful biological diversity of life, expressed in all its detail and species, as well as the maintenance of the integrity and good of the earth itself. This must come first and take priority over everything else. It's the final, decisive step away from anthropocentrism to biocentrism and geocentrism. This immediately places us in a humbler perspective; we are not separate from and over and against the world, but an intimate part of it. The cosmos is larger than us and we must take it seriously and recognize its autonomy. 'It would also be mistaken to view other living beings as mere objects subjected to arbitrary human domination ... The ultimate purpose of other creatures is not to be found in us,' LS says. Despite its limitations, in one extraordinary encyclical Francis shifts the focus away from us to the natural world where it belongs.

The final chapter of LS is a profound meditation on the Christian contribution to ecological spirituality with Francis highlighting the call to 'ecological conversion.' He says this conversion 'entails gratitude and gratuitousness, a recognition that the world is God's loving gift ... [and] a loving awareness that we are not disconnected from the rest of creatures, but joined in a splendid universal communion.' *'A splendid universal communion'*: that is the key to the moral principle this book tries to articulate. The whole of creation, including humankind, lives in communion and all creatures need each other. The world is not here just to support humankind; it is here for all of us.

Can we hope?

I've kept returning to the question: are there any grounds for hope, given that all the factual, statistical, intellectual, demographic and scientific arguments about overpopulation and the consequences for the environment and biodiversity seem to have so little impact on most people? A key reason for this is that we have lost the ability to deal with big stories or narratives and overpopulation is the biggest story of all. Our ethical systems, including non-religious, secular ethics, are still far too preoccupied with individualistic issues and emphases.

This where faith and religion can enter the picture. As we've seen, up until now religion has been largely absent from the discussion of ecology, global warming and population because it has been so besotted with the pathos of the human. But this is beginning to change quickly as Pope Francis, *Laudato Si'*, Orthodox Patriarch Bartholomew and several contemporary theologians have shown. In the years since LS was published, the environment, global warming and the loss of biodiversity have become central issues in Catholic theology, morality and life. The encyclical is not just a nod in the direction of ecology, but is a radical and revolutionary rethink of Christian theology and anthropocentrism in the light of the environmental crisis. And this has happened very quickly. Ecology was hardly ever mentioned in the Catholic church when I published *God's Earth. Religion as if matter really mattered* in 1995 and the book was then seen as revolutionary. At that time the number of Catholic thinkers who were addressing environmental issues could literally be counted on one hand and almost all of them were in the English or German-speaking world. In the twenty years between 1995 and 2015 ecological theology had gone from being a backwater issue in Catholicism to become a papal priority in *Laudato Si'*.

It is true that the theological foundation for ecological theology had been laid years before by theologians like the Austrian Jesuit, Karl Rahner and the German Protestant Jurgen Moltmann. Rahner saw the entire created cosmos as pervaded by God's grace with the whole of creation oriented in its inner core towards transcendence. Thus, the world becomes, in a literal sense, a sacrament or symbol of the presence of God, a 'mysterious infinity' where transcendence is to be discovered. This vision laid the foundation for seeing the whole of the created cosmos as a revelation of God.[143]

Now you don't have to be religious or even agree with religion to see that if this theology can influence just some of the world's 1.3 billion Catholics, let alone the world's 2.38 billion Christians, to think of the world in this way, then you have won a lot of people over to your side. People with strong religious convictions can be very powerful and influential when they are motivated by deep convictions and there is no doubt that for mainstream Catholics and Christians the earth and biodiversity are now moral imperatives. As Patriarch Bartholomew says ecology is not only a 'spiritual responsibility', but a *moral* imperative. Environmental destruction and extinction are serious sins, 'mortal sins' in Catholic rhetoric. This motivates believers to place a strongly positive value on creation and helps them resist the destructive tendencies to use and abuse nature that you find in all of us. The hopeful sign is that ecological awareness is already influencing the mainstream churches. No, it is not a priority among evangelicals and fundamentalists, but it is important for the top leadership of Catholicism, Eastern Orthodoxy and Protestantism. In the long-term, these are the churches that influence intelligent believers.

Sure, this has not yet explicitly extended to the population question, but that is also true of society generally. As we have seen, it is difficult to get this question onto society's agenda, resulting in politicians and decision makers avoiding the issue. It is here that the churches just might make a difference. The key shift is the outright rejection of anthropocentrism by Pope Francis. This is certainly going to influence Catholic and other Christian thinkers and it will gradually permeate through the church. This clears the way for the emphasis to shift to an ethic centred on the earth and biodiversity. Once that is established, the question of the priority of the human comes into focus and believers will come to see anthropocentrism for what it is, a particularly distorted heresy. This may happen quickly and surprize us.

Above all, faith offers purpose and meaning; existence is not just a fruitless exercise. Believers trust that as creator, God will not abandon the world. In a way, the most important virtue here is not faith, but hope and trust. Hope in this sense is not just wishful thinking, a kind of desperate desire that somehow things will work out, that they'll be OK. It is a dynamic reality that is motivated by a strong determination not to let those hell-bent on economic growth have their way, no matter what the cost to the environment and biodiversity. It is rooted in the kind of deep conviction that never surrenders. Reality is full of unexpected turns and twists, what we call serendipity, the kind of change that comes in the least expected way from unpredicted sources and angles.

We started this chapter with Lyn White's accusation that Christianity was the most anthropocentric religion in human history. There was some truth to that when he wrote it in 1967, but Pope Francis has given the lie to it in *Laudato Si'*. It is now incumbent on all Catholics, in fact on everyone who values life in all its forms, to embrace the humility of accepting the fact that we humans don't constitute the entire meaning of the history of the cosmos and the world. We are just part of nature, inextricably tried to every other living thing through our biological connectedness to the whole of reality. What needs to happen is that Christianity becomes a very powerful force in maintaining precisely the values that Lyn White treasured.

11

So Where to from Here?

Changing our priorities

The primary challenge facing us as humankind is changing our priorities from a myopic focus on ourselves as the unique source of meaning and purpose for the world, to a humbler recognition that we only make sense within the context of a larger whole, the earth, our only home. Our new morality prioritising the natural world will not only demand of us genuine humility, but also a generosity of spirit and a bigness of mind and heart that will test all that is best in us as persons. It doesn't mean that we will all have to become Francis of Assisi, or Mahatma Gandhi, or Greta Thunberg, or the indigenous Guajajara 'women warriors' of north-eastern Brazil protecting the 173,000 hectares (428,000 acres) of the primary rainforest that is their home from loggers. But it does mean that we have will have to take stands that defend the integrity of the earth and the environment and to assert that the protection of nature takes priority in every human decision.

That said, we would be fooling ourselves if we don't understand that this change will demand gargantuan re-adjustments on our part. The resistance to putting earth first will be massive. Much of it will focus on the human price to be paid, things like the loss of jobs, hindering 'development', the claim that whole groups of people will be marginalized, the loss of income, the lowering of standards of living, an endless litany of human pathos and threats to life as we know it. But it is precisely life as we know it that is the problem and that has to change. What we desperately need to do is to help people recover the broader, whole world vision we have articulated in order for us to build an ethical structure that takes the integrity and good of the earth and all its creatures into account while helping people deal with the difficult moral issues that flow from our principle of earth first, let alone the depopulation imperative.

Because we have difficulty with long term thinking, we easily succumb to what are really 'magical' solutions. One of the most potent magical solutions is one I mentioned earlier: that no matter what the problem, we implicitly believe that technology will somehow solve it, even if technology caused the problem in the first place. As futurist Kevin Kelly, *Wired* magazine founder, put it: 'The solution for technology problems, will be more technology; and if that causes other problems, the solution for those will be the same, more technology.'[144] This is symptomatic of the myth that if there's a problem with the world, technology will solve it because there is techno-solution for everything.

Pope Francis has little patience for this attitude. His blunt critique of technology in *Laudato si'* is based on the writings of the theologian Romano Guardini who was critical of the way technology cuts us off from nature by creating an artificial, abstract, one-dimensional, de-personalized and manipulative world. Pope Francis links his critique of technology to an extractive mentality that presupposes that 'there is an infinite supply of the earth's goods, and this leads to the planet being squeezed dry beyond every limit', an idea, he says, that 'proves so attractive to economists, financiers and experts in technology'. He says that 'technology tends to absorb everything into its ironclad logic' and promises 'quick fixes' which favour 'the interests of certain powerful groups'.

Another who understood the impact of technology was the German philosopher, Martin Heidegger (1889–1976). His attachment to Nazism is well known and the publication of his *Black Notebooks* has now revealed his anti-Semitism.[145] Despite this, I believe that he still has much to contribute to contemporary debate about the future. While he was not an environmentalist in the contemporary sense, his later thought expressed profound ambiguity about the technological culture we have inherited from Western science.

His 1962 essay *The Question Concerning Technology* is truly prophetic.[146] When he talks about technology, Heidegger is not talking about particular technologies, but is actually referring to a mindset, an attitude to reality, whereby we think we can manipulate everything for our own use, including even ourselves. He is referring to the human tendency to interfere through mechanistic force or artificial manipulation in the natural dynamics of the world, to use nature for some perceived 'good' for humankind. We seemingly can't leave anything alone; we even play with the genetic structure of our own bodies and, in artificial intelligence, replace our own minds with machines that mimic our thought processes to solve problems. We are dominated and driven by a kind of opportunistic, 'can-do' mentality; if something can be done, it should be done. It needs no further ethical justification.

The deep root of this, according to Heidegger, is our manipulative attitude toward nature. Like the econometric mindset, he sees the technological mindset as built into the very structure of modern thinking. It so possesses our intellectual horizons and so penetrates the way we perceive reality that we are almost unable to think outside a technological context. Our unquestioned, instinctual reaction to nature is that it must be managed, improved upon, or used. A kind of measuring, calculating, use-oriented, management-style logic is applied to everything. Heidegger says we are so trapped in this attitude that it is almost impossible for us to view reality differently.

I'm not saying that specific technologies are bad. I am writing this text on a computer, I drive a car, I fly in airplanes, I use social media and electrical appliances make our home liveable. What Heidegger is trying to get at is the way in which a kind of unconscious techno-management mentality dominates us and provides the basic paradigm through which we instinctively view reality and ourselves. This mentality objectifies everything, including the natural world, and it now so dominates our mental horizon and so impregnates our attitudes that we cannot avoid being unconsciously immersed in it and influenced by it. Technology creates a normative way of viewing nature, whereby we see the world as resources that we can unlock, exploit, or store for later use. As a philosopher Heidegger is not so much interested in the instruments we use, as in a technological *attitude* that nowadays dominates the way in which we frame our approach to reality.

He says that since the scientific revolution, we have lost our sense of wonder and relate to nature primarily as a reality we understand, classify and name, seeing it a source of energy and resources. Technology, he says, creates a cultural and intellectual *Gestell*, or way of 'en-framing' reality, that unconsciously determines the way we think. And for Heidegger *how* we think, the processes and parameters of our thought, are far more important than *what* we think, the content of our thought. As a result, we live in a kind of technological trance. What Heidegger wants to do is to transcend this attitude by thinking completely outside the dominating techno-paradigm, to recover a tradition of thinking which had not lost an organic connection with existence in the natural world. He wants us to think outside the accepted conventions and to move into an alternative space where we view reality from a completely different perspective. He wants to shock us out of our predetermined and unconscious ways of thinking, so that our imaginations are opened to new ways of perceiving reality. To do this we will have to escape our fixation on dominating and exploiting the world and enter into a new moral universe, that of putting nature and the world first rather than ourselves. Heidegger would have a deep sympathy with the basic principle that this book has articulated.

Heidegger argues that we have reached the tag-end of the old philosophy, the philosophy started by Socrates, Plato and Aristotle, which is simply the expression of the unconscious dominance of an exploitative, calculating, mechanized, efficiency-oriented mentality applied to everything. We implicitly and unconsciously define ourselves over and against the natural world which, Heidegger says, we have reduced to a *Bestand*, a 'standing reserve' of resources and energy to be exploited for our needs, without regard for what we now call the broader ecological context. He points out that nowadays we even view ourselves as a kind of 'standing reserve' which can be manipulated and exploited through genetic engineering, in vitro fertilization, the manipulation our DNA and ultimately through artificial intelligence.

In an ironic twist, Heidegger argues that the issues surrounding technology and our divorce from the natural world are not *ethical* problems. In the final analysis we can't deal with the destructive results of technology by acting ethically. This is not an issue which can be 'managed' by goodness. What we need is a new paradigm, a whole new way of thinking and viewing reality. That is exactly what our principle of the priority of nature does. What we have to do is to see the natural world not from the perspective of what it can do for us, but from the deeper perspective of its value in itself, in the fact that it exists. If we are able to achieve that then there is hope for our future. If not, the future will be a miserable dystopia.

Untergang

When I began this book, I never expected that we would be immersed in a worldwide and highly infectious pandemic before I finished it. It has given us a chance to rethink our whole approach to what is important in life and society, to review the neo-liberal market ideology that has dominated us for the last forty years. It has brough us to a decisive time, a critical moment of decision, what New Testament Greek calls καιρός, or 'kairos', the time when lurking and underlying problems come to a head and hard choices have to be made. It is also seen as a creative time of opportunity when we can set out on new and better ways. But it is also the time when disastrously wrong choices can be made. What the pandemic has done is to create a hiatus, a space within which we can reflect on our situation and see the result of our exploitative, anthropocentric attitude to nature and our out-of-control numbers.

In Heidegger's more negative rhetoric, the pandemic has brought about a dangerous situation that he called *Untergang*, literally a time of sinking, foundering, downfall and ruin. The meaning of the word was vividly illustrated in the graphic imagery of the 2004 German movie *Der Untergang* which depicts the Soviet siege of Berlin and the last days of Hitler in the Führer-bunker, leading up to 2 May 1945 when the centre of the city finally fell. The most striking part of the film is the utter denial of Hitler and his intimates about the chaos and death that is happening just a few hundred metres away from their cosseted world of the bunker. There is a sense in which we live in a similar unreal world as global warming and environmental *Untergang* occurs all around us, as we retreat into the total unreality of refusing to confront overpopulation, global warming and biodiversity loss.

Environmental *Untergang* demands a massive shift, not only

in moral reasoning, but in our approach to life. What is demanded is a profound change of perspective that prioritizes nature. We have to understand the deep interlocking of all life forms and come to a realization that without the complexity, beauty and sustainment provided by the natural world in all its diversity, complexity, wild otherness and feeling of transcendent presence, human life will degenerate into a meaningless, arid emptiness in a feed-lot world inhabited by ten or more billion robotic people who have lost the characteristics that make us human. This is the apocalyptic dystopia we face if we don't put nature first and confront overpopulation. The terrible danger is that in the face of this challenge, we will give up and surrender to the temptation to 'eat, drink and be merry, for tomorrow we die', a saying that comes originally from the Hebrew prophet Isaiah (22:13). The simple reality is that we have never been in this situation before; we don't know what to do and neither do the experts or so-called futurologists. We try to compartmentalize our situation, to get on with life and hope someone – anyone – will solve world problems. Heidegger foresaw the kind of situation in which we have now become entangled. In his own enigmatic way, I think he points to a way of escaping from it.

Before he died Heidegger gave an interview to the tabloid magazine *Der Spiegel*. The interview was published just after his death in 1976. The interviewer asked him a question about the state of things in the mid-1970s with the Cold War threatening nuclear annihilation. He asked: can we survive and save the world? Heidegger responded cryptically and in a typically round-about way, saying: 'Philosophy will be unable to effect any immediate change in the current state of the world. This is true not only of philosophy, but of all purely human reflection and endeavour. Only a god can save us. The only possibility available to us is that by thinking and poetizing we prepare a readiness for the appearance of a god … [because in] … the absence of a god … we are in a state of *Untergang*, foundering and ruin.'[147]

What is he saying? Putting it into contemporary terms, I think he is warning us that with overpopulation, global warming and biodiversity loss already realities, it follows that 'all merely human thought and endeavour', in other words philosophy, ethics and human action won't help because they are wedded to the old philosophical-exploitative

141

techno-paradigm. In this context he says, 'Only a god can save us.' Was this a conservative old man returning to the Catholicism of his youth? That is most unlikely because he considered the Judeo-Christian God and Christianity 'dead' in terms of any influence in the contemporary world. Who or what, then, is this 'god' that is meant to save us?

Firstly, I think he is trying to convey that the reversal called for in our attitude to the world is so profound that we will not be able to do it unaided. He told *Der Spiegel*: 'I know of no paths to the immediate transformation of the present situation of the world, assuming that such a thing is humanly possible at all.' He's saying that no matter what we do within our present philosophical and cultural structures, our attitude to nature will always be techno-exploitative. Even by acting ethically, for example by recycling, living simply, abandoning consumerism, individuals won't be able to achieve a transformation of the situation. The reason: what we are dealing with here is impersonal and inexorable, similar to what the German philosopher G.W.F. Hegel and later Karl Marx saw as the dialectic, or 'impersonal force' of history, whereby reality moved inexorably through deep underlying, deterministic processes over which individuals and communities had little or no influence. In other words, what happens on a macro scale is something beyond our personal or communal ability to change.

Here we need to remember that our human freedom is very limited. So much of our reality is determined by social and natural forces that are far beyond our personal control. Heidegger is arguing that a predominant social force is the way technology creates a very specific *Gestell* or 'thought-frame', or way of perceiving reality and viewing the world. If we understand this, then we can begin to identify and name our predicament. He also says we also need an attitude of *Bereitshaft*, meaning 'readiness' or 'being on stand-by'. There is an apocalyptic note in this, but perhaps this is precisely what is lacking in contemporary culture. We might act more quickly to deal with overpopulation, global warming and biodiversity loss if we recognized that that the world as we know it is on the edge of destruction and that what awaits us might well resemble the scenarios sketched-out in dystopic novels previously mentioned.

However, we are not totally powerless. Heidegger says we have two powers or processes at our disposal: 'thinking' and 'poetising'. These words suggest that we can begin to conceive of reality in a different way, as we try to imagine new and different possibilities. By thinking, we will come to understand our predicament and by poetizing we will develop our imaginations so that we will be able to perceive the actual presence of this saving 'god'. The mature Heidegger had moved decisively in the direction of mysticism and, in fact, much of his later thought is close to the German Dominican mystic, Meister Eckhart (c.1260–1327) whom he often quotes.

Essentially, I see Heidegger's philosophy as extremely suggestive in that it points towards new ideas and asks us to interpret and explore them for ourselves. As Heidegger scholar Thomas Sheehan points out, at the core of his philosophy is the concept of Being (with a capital B) and no one really understands exactly what he meant by the word, which frees us to explore the idea ourselves.[148] In my view Heidegger uses Being as a way of talking about the Transcendent, the 'god' of the *Der Spiegel* interview, not the conventionally religious, up-in-heaven, constantly interfering deity of the pentecostal 'God-botherers', but more the hidden, lurking-present God of the mystics. The *Der Spiegel* passage conveys a sense that this transcendent presence will come, that the passionate force of Being will conquer the non-existence of technology, environmental vandalism and destruction.

Heidegger is saying that what we need to develop is our poetic side rather than our rational. By 'poetizing' he means using our imaginations. Imagination is absolutely central to human existence. It is the dynamic process whereby we make connections between realities that at first sight seem unconnected. Looking at it another way, imagination is the dynamic energy whereby we draw on our senses, life histories, feelings, thinking faculties, powers of inference, and all our life-lessons to make images and to filter and sort out all the material we experience into a meaningful pattern. The American theologian, William F. Lynch, says that imagination 'is not a separate or single faculty. It is all our resources, all our faculties, our whole history, our whole life and our whole heritage, all brought to bear upon the concrete world inside and outside the self, to form images of the world, and thus to find it, cope with it, shape it, even make it. The task of the imagination is to imagine the real.'[149] For Lynch 'the real' is the material world. He says that we have far too superficial a conception of earth and the cosmos. It has, as he says, 'infinite depth'. It is a permeable reality through which we can grasp images of what he calls the 'next world', the 'transcendent' or the 'sacred', perhaps what Heidegger would call 'god'. When our imaginations are stultified, we descend into various levels of unreality, even madness, and there is a sense in which insanity is a total loss of imagination; in truth a madman is a person imprisoned in a myopic, unilateral vision, unable to conceive of anything different.

So 'the ability to poetise', by which Heidegger means the ability to see things differently and escape being trapped by the conventional, is centrally important. People who refuse to act, who bury their heads in the sand, who compartmentalise their lives and focus on parochial and familial self-interest, persuade themselves that we can do nothing about the problems we face. Or they see these as long-term problems that, fingers crossed, might never eventuate, just like people never expected a pandemic, despite the predictions of experts for decades. People become imprisoned in a kind of here-and-now situation to which there is no possible alternative. In contrast, those who can poetise have the ability to embrace alternative ways of seeing reality; they will not succumb to the inevitable. They understand that the fundamental principle is the priority of the integrity of the earth and biodiversity.

The massive challenge that faces us is to move from our abstract, exploitative, manipulative, economistic vision of the world, to one that sees the world as an evolving community of living beings who are not mere cannon fodder for our needs and demands, but have a value and existence completely other than us and independent of us. In other words, we have to begin to perceive elements of personhood, or what the visionary priest and palaeontologist, Pierre Teilhard de Chardin calls 'consciousness', throughout the world and at the very heart of evolution itself. For Teilhard, incipient consciousness, the key characteristic of personhood, is there from the beginning and is present in all creatures. But Teilhard goes even further, seeing consciousness in all of the material realities, the matter that makes-up the earth. In a sense, we already recognize this consciousness with companion animals; we acknowledge them as personal presences in our lives. But this also has to extend to wild animals, to species we

144

don't control. They too have personhood and, as such, have rights inherent in themselves.

Indigenous peoples understand animal personhood perfectly well because they live their lives in a natural world of symbols. Their experiences emphasize the deeper sacramental, symbolic nature of reality, rather than our superficially Western rational-scientific explanation of it. Essentially, they have no concept of nature as an impersonal, neutral reality, as we have in Western thought. For example, native Americans, like the Ojibwe of the north-eastern woodlands of North America, believe that there are many other-than-human-persons who, like us, have causative agency in the world. They regard all sentient creatures as having self-awareness and an understanding of their circumstances. Anthropologist and folklorist, A. Irving Hallowell, writes that native North Americans believe that they can talk with sentient animals, what he called 'other-than-human-persons'. He says that 'they have personal identity, autonomy, and volition'.[150] In this context, the natural world takes on a whole assembly of personal meanings and presences that we Westerners simply don't experience, except perhaps in our relationship with domestic animals.

Here I am not suggesting that we jettison our Western intellectual and cultural tradition because we still have pervasive remnants of this notion of the personhood of nature in our own tradition: we refer to nature in the feminine as 'mother earth'. We have our own spiritual tradition of oneness with the natural world and its creatures, the kind of approach symbolised by Saint Francis of Assisi with his love of animals and his ability to communicate with them. Francis was not some type of romantic, sentimental new age guru, but an ascetic in the Catholic tradition who saw it as his task to rebuild the church. We also have the Celtic spiritual tradition. The early Irish Christians loved the world, but they never romanticized it. They lived in close contact with nature, experiencing 'the world of wildlife, trees, plants and forces of weather, the sea and the vast starry sky as manifestations of God's creative nature, a sacrament of divine presence'.[151] The Irish saints also had a love for animals, especially those that were hunted or endangered, like wolves and bears. They particularly loved isolated places that were difficult to access, like mountain tops and inaccessible islands like Skellig Michael, a rock pinnacle rising 281 metres out of the Atlantic Ocean, just off the Kerry coast.

Solutions?

All of this adds up to a fundamental challenge of central importance for us and the future of the earth itself. Here I need to ask patience from empiricist, fact-based readers, because I am suggesting that, *pace* science, we have to look beyond the scientific paradigm for an answer. What I am asking is: is there a conscious presence or reality out there, something resembling Lovelock's Gaia, that is already re-acting to the pressures that human overpopulation is placing upon nature? Perceptive people, many of them non-religious, who have experienced the wilderness, also speak of a 'presence' that they intuit lurking in unexpected places in nature, leading sometimes to an ecstatic experience of self-transcendence. World-renowned Tasmanian wilderness photographer, Peter Dombrovskis, simply says: 'When you go out there, you don't get away from it all. You get back to it all. You come home to what's important. You come home to yourself.'

But it is not just the disappearance of wilderness and beauty that's the problem. There is also a barrier to the apprehension of transcendent presence built into modern life itself. We are pragmatic and phlegmatic in our approach to virtually everything and our minds are so analytically focused that it has become almost impossible for us to, as Heidegger says, 'poetise'. We have divided up the natural world and analysed its component parts and estimated their economic value. We have expelled from our mental horizons any sense of iconographic mystery in nature. Loggers, miners, industrial agriculturalists and other sundry exploiters of nature are crudely pragmatic and focus entirely on the amount of 'product' they can extract from nature. It is a prime example of the cultural autism that characterises our society and neo-rationalist economics.

At first sight I may have seemed to have wandered right off topic and lost my focus on depopulation. However, I have purposely developed this notion of the natural world as a community of personal presences, because it is only when we embrace this that we will begin to actualize our basic principle that the natural world takes priority, and the priority of nature is intimately interlocked with the question of overpopulation. The reason why we have to reduce our numbers is to care for the environment and biodiversity; the more people there are, the greater our impact on nature. These issues are intimately interconnected when you put earth first.

So, where are we now in terms of the future? The answer: at an absolutely critical point in human and earth history, a real καιρός, or *Untergang*. The decisions we take now regarding climate change, species loss, the use of non-renewable resources, will decide the future of humankind, and the kind of earth on which we might or might not survive. Sure, we are slowing the rate of population growth and we know that eventually we will reach some type of equilibrium. But that is not enough. The optimum number of people on earth is probably at the absolute outside three billion, preferably less, most of them living in efficient cities. Currently this presumes a population shrinkage of around 4.8 billion. Every other scenario leads to slow-motion disasters involving widespread starvation, breakdowns in water supplies and a struggle to the death for ever scarcer basic resources.

Here it is important to reject the blandishments of fantasists who try to convince us that the more people we have, the more brains we'll have to solve our problems, or others who assure us that technology will supply all the answers. The simple reality is: the world is massively over-populated *now*, global warming is impacting us *now*, a massive extinction process is under-way *now*, we are chewing-up an earth and a half of resources *now*. The earth might survive this, but we most probably won't, and even if we did it make it into the future, it will be an ugly, truncated existence for the human remnant. What are we going to do?

First, we have to recover the sense that nature is not only a living organism, but that we are part of it and have no existence outside of it. It is where we evolved and where we belong. Even more than that, it is sacred in the sense that it exudes a sense or feeling of transcendent presence and it nurtures our imaginations. As a result, we have to abandon the notion that the world is a mere source of raw resources for our use. Second, we will have to change some of our engrained mindsets. Among these is the technological mindset which is closely allied to the econometric mindset which, in turn, is intimately linked to neo-liberal, capitalist ideology. All of these interconnected and toxic myths must be jettisoned in order to clear the way for us to adopt our fundamental moral and ethical principle: that the integrity of the earth and its species comes before everything else. This must be the fundamental norm for all our future decisions, whatever the human consequences. This doesn't mean we abandon those people impacted by the changes that earth first requires. In the vast majority of cases solutions can be found that don't create impossible difficulties for them. The wider community must step in to help these people adapt.

On the broader international scale, the developed world must assist developing countries reduce their populations through education and medical and reproductive services for women. Where there is resistance, the international community needs to apply pressure, so that women in developing countries are provided with on-going education, family planning and reproductive health services, so they can make responsible decisions regarding their fertility. Cultural and religious opposition to population control has to be confronted by the higher moral demand of the good of all creation.

Having said all that, the situation regarding world population still seems hopeless. How do we depopulate, get back quickly to a position in which we have a manageable and sustainable number of people, given the damage we are already doing to the earth? To be honest, as I come to the end of this book and having looked at the evidence, I must admit I don't have an immediate answer, short of nuclear war or a catastrophic pandemic, which would certainly massively reduce population, but which would be horrendous and beyond moral justification. And after the catastrophe what would we be left with? A world with a small population, but probably much worse than any scenario imagined by dystopian novelists.

Whatever the solution, everything must be negotiated in light of the absolutely fundamental moral value of the good of earth and its species. The key word here is negotiated. What we're involved in is balancing a set of conflicting moral principles. Moral decision-making always involves grey areas, compromise and finding a way through moral conundrums. Also, such decision-making involves a hierarchy of moral values; some are more important than others. I would argue that the fundamental principle of earth first means that the integrity of the environment, dealing with global warming and protecting other species from extinction, must come before everything else. This makes sense even from an anthropocentric viewpoint, because we want to maintain a liveable world for our children and grand-children.

While I am deeply committed to the principle of earth first and I don't resile from that, I also see the dangers of a kind of lurking fascism, a kind of ruthless willingness to sacrifice the weakest people to create some type of idealized world. While we must retreat from anthropocentrism, that doesn't mean we strip vulnerable people of their rights and dignity. No, I'm not backing-off from what I have said previously, but I am trying to maintain perspective. You don't deal with one extreme by going to the other. Yes, the situation we face is dire and we are going to have to get very, very tough with ourselves and with those unwilling to change. But we must never abandon the genuine values and principles that our culture and civilization have brought us.

In the end it is those who are determined to act, who have not retreated to denial, or who refuse to give-in to the kind of myopia and narrow parochialism that puts self-interest before everything else, who really keep hope alive. Clearly there are grounds for a sense of hopelessness. How can we reduce human numbers while respecting human dignity? How can we go from almost eight billion to a sustainable number quickly, short of nuclear war, or an utterly catastrophic pandemic, or a complete collapse in male sperm counts? Should we be willing to compromise traditional human values to protect the world? Is human dignity so sacred that it takes priority in every circumstance? Difficult as they are, these are the kinds of questions that now confront us, and solutions don't come easily.

With cynicism a real temptation, the one thing we have to hang onto is hope. Hope is not some nebulous reality that sorts things out without any effort from us. It involves a determination not to give up, not to surrender to pessimism. Essentially, hope is the ability to see things differently; it involves an activation of the imagination, the facility to discover new ways of viewing reality, the capacity to create new and different possibilities, to make unexpected connections. Reality is full of serendipity, of unexpected twists and turns. Change often comes in the least expected way from unpredicted sources and angles.

Perhaps nature might make the decisions for us. Coming as I do from the Catholic tradition my ultimate hope is that God will not abandon a commitment to the world. As John's gospel says: 'God so loved the world that he gave his only son … so that the world might be saved through him' (3:16-17). No, I'm not calling for some kind of magical divine intervention. But as I have suggested, I believe there is a close connection between God and the natural world and it may well be nature itself that acts to reign-in our excesses.

Whatever happens, we are in a truly unique situation which will call for all our creative resources. We are going to need all of the imaginative power that went into constructing all that is best in our culture, and then some. The alternative is too terrible to contemplate.

Notes

Chapter 1

1   Keith Somerville, 'Why it's not all about security as West beefs up military in Africa's Sahel', *The Conversation*, 27 October 2016 and 'Explainer: the role of foreign military forces in Niger', *The Conversation*, 9 September 2018; and Krishnadev Calamur, 'The Region Where ISIS, al-Qaeda and Boko Haram Converge', *The Atlantic*, 5 October 2017.

2   Jill Filipovic, *The Guardian*, 16 March 2017.

Chapter 2

3   Martin Luther King in a speech to Planned Parenthood, 5 May 1966.

4   *Radio Times*, 22 January 2013.

5   Paul Collins, *God's Earth. Religion as if matter really mattered*, HarperCollins, 1995. 1.

6   George Monbiot, 'Neoliberalism – the ideology at the root of all our problems', *The Guardian*, 15 April 2016.

7   Max Roser, 'Twice as Long—life expectancy round the world', *Our World in Data*, 8 October 2018.

Chapter 3

8   David Owen, *Thylacine. The Tragic Tale of the Tasmanian Tiger*, 2003, 7.

9   Robert Paddle, *The Last Tasmania Tiger. The history and Extinction of the Thylacine*, 2000, 237.

10   Barry Yeoman, 'Why the Passenger Pigeon Went Extinct', *Audubon Magazine*, May–June 2014 at www.audubon.org/magazine/may-june-2014/why-passenger-pigeon-went-extinct

11   Ibid.

12   Gilbert King, 'Where the Buffalo No Longer Roamed', *Smithsonian*,

17 July 2012 at www.smithsonianmag.com/history/where-the-buffalo-no-longer-roamed-3067904/

13   Edward O. Wilson, *The Future of Life*, 2002, 92. *Half-Earth: Our Planet's Fight for Life*, 2016, 38–39.

14   Wilson, *Future*, 94–95.

15   John Man, *Atlas of the Year 1000*, 1999, 131.

16   Tim Flannery, *The Future Eaters. An ecological history of the Australasian lands and people*, 1994.

17   Richard E. Leakey and Roger Lewin, *People of the Lake. Mankind and Its Beginnings*, 1978, 254.

18   A.J. McMichael, *Planetary Overload. Global Environmental Change and the Health of the Human Species*, 1993, 34.

19   McMichael, *Overload*, 105 and 82–3.

20   Paul Martin, *Twilight of the Mammoths: ice age extinctions and rewilding America*, 2005.

21   Chris Clarkson et al., 'Human occupation of northern Australia by 65,000 years ago', *Nature*, 19 July 2017. See also *The Conversation*, 20 July 2017.

22   Sander van der Kaars et al., 'Humans rather than climate the primary cause of Pleistocene megafaunal extinction in Australia', *Nature Communications*, 20 January 2017.

23   Simon Worrall, 'When did the First Americans Arrive? Its' complicated', *National Geographic*, 9 June 2018.

24   Golson, Jack et al, *Ten Thousand Years of Cultivation at Kuk Swamp in the Highlands of Papua-New Guinea* at https://press.anu.edu/publications/series/terra-australia/ten-thousand-years-cultivation-kuk-swamp-highlands-papua-new

25   Colin McEvedy and Richard Jones, *Atlas of World Population History*, 1978, 13–15. Another historical demographer, Ralph Thomlinson, cites higher figures.

26   McEvedy and Jones, *Atlas*, 171, 343.

27   McEvedy and Jones, *Atlas*, 171.

28   Peter Brown, *The World of Late Antiquity*,1989, 122.

29   McEvedy and Jones, *Atlas*, 18.

30   Paul Collins, *The Birth of the West. Rome, Germany, France and the Creation of Europe in the Tenth Century*, 2013.

31   Thomas Malthus, *An Essay on the Principle of Population*, 1803 edition, London: J.M. Dent, 2, 195.

32   John Vidal, 'Cut world population and redistribute resources, expert urges', *The Guardian*, 26 April 2012 and 'World needs to stabilise population and cut consumption, says Royal Society', *The Guardian*, 26 April 2012

33   Qing Ke et al., 'China's shift from population control to population quality. Implications for Neurology' at www.ncbi.nlm.nib.gov/pmc/articles/PMC4999320/

34   Matthew Connelly, *Fatal Misconception. The struggle to control world population*, 2008.

35   International Union for Conservation of Nature, Red List, 'Species Extinction – The Facts'.

Chapter 4

36   Australian Greens at www.greens.org.au/policy/population

37   Paul and Anne Ehrlich, *The Population Explosion*, New York, Simon and Schuster, 1990, 21, 32.

38   Andrew Glikson, 'The methane time bomb', *Energy Procedia*, 146(2018), 23–29.

39   Australian Bureau of Meteorology and CSIRO 'State of the Climate Report', November 2020.

40   Lee Kump and Michael Mann, *Dire Predictions. A Visual Guide to the Finding of the IPCC*, 2015.

41   www.worldometers.info/world-population/kiribati-population/

42   Quotations from Journeyman Pictures, 'The Tropical Paradise Being Swallowed by the Pacific'. See https://www.journeyman.tv/film/7382

43   Ibid.

44   https.//www.unhcr.org/figures-at-a-glance.html

45   *Forbes*, 1 February 2017.

46 *Daily Mail,* 11 March 2011.

47 *Radio Times,* 22 January 2013.

48 *The Independent,* 30 December 2014.

49 *War on Waste,* ABC TV, 2018, episodes 1 and 2.

50 Paul Ehrlich and Anne Ehrlich, 'It's the numbers, stupid!' in Goldie, Jenny and Betts, Katherine, *Sustainable Futures,* 2014, 1.

51 *Business Insider,* 28 August 2016.

52 *The Economist,* 11 January 2018.

Chapter 5

53 Sean McDonagh, 'Genetic Engineering is not the Answer', *America,* 2 May 2005.

54 Columban Mission Society, *Unjust Genes – Life and Death for Sale,* a DVD and booklet on genetically engineered food. At www.columban. org.au

55 David Emerson, 'Biogenic Iron Dust. A novel approach to ocean iron fertilization as a means of large-scale removal of carbon dioxide from the atmosphere', *Frontiers in Marine Science,* 7 February 2019.

56 Al Gore, *Earth in the Balance: Forging a New Common Purpose, 1992,* 307.

57 Jane O'Sullivan, 'Silver tsunami or silver lining', SPA Discussion Paper, October 2020.

58 ABC News, 27/4/2020. At www.abc.net.au/news/2020-04-27/ demographer-warns-of-missing-children-of-covid-19/12187262.

59 Carole Dalin et al., 'Groundwater depletion embedded in international food trade', *Nature,* 543(2017), 700–704.

60 Gro Harlem Brndtland, 'Report of World Commission on Environment and Development: Our Common Future' at www.un-documents.net/our-common-future.pdf

61 Optimum Population Trust, 'Modest Footprint Carrying Capacity as calculated from Ecological Footprints of Nations Data; Calculations of Human Population Sustainability by countries' at www. optimumpopulation.org. For current populations numbers I have

used the webpage Worldometer at www.worldometers.info/world-population

62   G.C. Daily, Anne and Paul Ehrlich, 'Optimum Population Size', *Population and Environment*, 15(1994), 469–475.

63   Australian Academy of Science at www.science.org.au/curious/earth/how-many-people-can-earth-actually-support

64   Joel E. Cohen, *How Many People Can the Earth Support?* 1995.

Chapter 6

65   Thomas Berry, *The Dream of the Earth*, 1988, 14.

66   Author interview with Berry ABC Radio National, *Insights*, 27 January 1991.

67   Thomas Berry, 'Contemporary spirituality: the journey of the human community', *Cross Currents*, Summer/Fall 1974, 174–75.

68   Philip Rieff, *The Triumph of the Therapeutic. The Uses of Faith after Freud*, 1966.

69   See endnote 66.

Chapter 7

70   Asoka Bandarage, 'Control cash not people', *Ecologist*, 38/8, October 2008.

71   Wang Fang, 'The End of China's One-Child Policy', *Studies in Family Planning*, 30 March 2016.

72   William H. McNeill, *Population and Politics since 1750*, 1990, 58.

73   K.H. Connell, *The Population of Ireland, 1750–1845*, 1950, 58–59.

74   Rand Corporation (2002), 'International Family Planning Programs: Criticisms and Responses' at www.rand.org/pubs/research_briefs/RB5063/index1.html

75   Gilles Pison, 'Is the Earth over-populated?' The Conversation (Australia) 31 October 2017 at www.theconversation.com/is-the-earth-overpopulated-86555

76   Daniel Bricker and John Ibbitson, *Empty Planet. The Shock of Global*

Population Decline, 2019.

77   David Herlihy, *The Black Death and the Transformation of the West*, 1997; Susan Scott & Christopher Duncan, *Return of the Black Death, 2003*.

78   John M. Barry, *The Great Influenza. The Story of the Deadliest Pandemic in History*, 2005.

79   John F. Brundage and G. Dennis Shanks, 'Deaths from Bacterial Pneumonia during 1918–19 Influenza Pandemic', *Emerging Infectious Diseases Journal*, Vol 14, no 8, August 2008.

80   Robin McKie, 'Scientists trace 2002 Sars virus to colony of cave-dwelling bats in China', *The Guardian*, 10 December 2017.

81   BBC, 10/7/2021.

82   Edward Holmes, 'COVID-19: Time is now to prepare for the next coronavirus outbreak', 9 April 2020 at www.sydney.edu.au/news-opinion/news/2020/04/09

83   Hagai Levine et al., 'Temporal trends in sperm count: a systematic review and mega-regression analysis', *Human Reproduction Update*, 23(2017), 646–659 at www.ncbi.nih.gov/pubmed/28981654

84   Pallay Sengupta et al., 'Evidence in decreasing sperm count in African population from 1965 to 2015', *African Health Sciences*, 17(2017), 418–427.

85   Attenborough, 'Human are a plague on the earth', *Radio Times*, 22/1/2013.

86   *The Australian*, 16 June 2010.

87   *The Guardian*, 29 June 2019.

88   *The Guardian*, 23 April 2019.

89   Ibid.

Chapter 8

90   Collins, *Birth of West*, 19–20.

91   Roger Lovegrove, *Silent Fields: The long decline of a nation's wildlife*, 2007, 24–26.

92   Theodore Roosevelt, African Game Trails; An Account of the African Wanderings of an American Hunter-Naturalist, 1909, 90. For the number

of animals killed see 457–459.

93   www.wwf.org.uk/updates/libing-planet-report-2018

94   www.worldwildlife.org/pages/living-planet-report-2014

95   www.worldwildlife.org/pages/living-planet-report-2016

96   International Union for Conservation of Nature, Red List, 'Species Extinction – The Facts' at www.iucn.org/resources/conservation-tools/ icun-red-list-threatened-species

97   John Woinarski et al., 'A hidden toll: Australia's cats kill about 650 million reptiles a year', *The Conversation*, 26 June 2018.

98   Paul Collins, *Burn. The epic story of bushfire in Australia,* 62 and passim.

99   Chris Dickman, *News and Opinion*, University of Sydney, 8 January 2020.

100   National Wildlife Foundation, *Reversing America's Wildlife Crisis*, 29 March 2018 at www.nwf.org/ReversingWildlifeCrisis

101   United Nations, Sustainable Development Goals, Press Release, 'UN Report: Nature's Dangerous Decline "Unprecedented"; Species Extinction Rates "Accelerating"', 6 May 2019.

102   E.O. Wilson in *The New York Times*, 12 March 2016.

103   E.O Wilson in Tony Hill, 'Can the World Really Set Aside Half of the Planet for Wildlife?' *Smithsonian*, September 2014.

104   Gary Polakovic, 'Water dispute on the Nile River could destabilize the region', *USC News*, 13 July 2021

105   World Wildlife Fund, *Living Planet Report 2018* at www. worldwildlife.org/pages/living-planet-report-2018

Chapter 9

106   Kari Norgaard, *Living in Denial: Climate Change, Emotions and Everyday Life*, 2011. See also https://vimeo.com/85591316

107   Ernest Becker, *The Denial of Death*, 1973, ix.

108   Sigmund Freud, *Group Psychology and the Analysis of the Ego*, 1965, 16.

109   Becker, *Death*, 133.

110   Ross Douthat, *The Decadent Society, How We Became the Victims of Our*

Own Success, 2020.

111   James Lovelock, *Gaia: A New Look at Life on Earth*, 1979.

112   James Lovelock, *The Revenge of Gaia: why the earth is fighting back – and how we can still save humanity,* 2007.

Chapter 10

113   *Standard Digital* (Kenyan newspaper), 13 January 2018.

114   Paul Collins, *Believers. Does Australian Catholicism Have a Future?* 2008, 43–46.

115   Historical   figures   from   www.worldometers.info/world. population/philippines-population/ or /Kenya-population/

116   John T. Noonan, *Contraception. A History of Its Treatment by the Catholic Theologians and Canonists*, 1968, 406.

117   Pew Research Center, 'The Changing Global Religious Landscape', 5 April 2017.

118   Quoted in Richard H. Schwartz, *Judaism and Global Survival*, 2002, 148.

119   American Jewish Committee, 'Prospecting the Jewish Future: Population Projections, 2000 – 2080', *American Jewish Year Book,* 2000, 103 –146.

120   Quoted in Judith Zimmerman and Barbara Trainin, ed., *Jewish Population*: *Renascence or Oblivion*, 1979, 42.

121   Basim Musallam in Warren T. Reich (ed), *The Encyclopedia of Bioethics*, 1978, III, 1268.

122   Michael Lipka and Conrad Hackett, 'Why Muslims are the world's fastest-growing religious group', Pew Research Center, 6 April 2017 at   www.pewresearch.org/fact-tank/2017/04/06/why-muslims-are-the-worlds-fastest-growing-religious-group

123   Lynn White, 'The Historical Roots of the Ecological Crisis', *Science*, 155(1967), 1203–1207.

124   Karl Barth, *Church Dogmatics*, III, Part 4, English trans, 1961, 273.

125   Nicon D. Patrinacos, *The Orthodox Church on Birth Control*, 1975, 46, 48.

126 Patriarch Bartholomew at www.patriarchiate.org/bartholomew-quotes

127 John Chryssavgis, 'The Green Patriarch', at www.patriarchate.org/the-green-patriarch

128 *Catholic News Service*, 16/10/2020.

129 Xavier Rynne, *The Third Session. The debates and decrees of Vatican Council II September 14 to November 21 1964*, 1965, 161, 162.

130 Hehir in Reich, *Encyclopedia of Ethics*, 3, 1254.

131 Paul VI, *Populorum Progressio*, 26 March 1967, 37.

132 For a critical treatment of John Paul II see Paul Collins, *Absolute Power. How the Pope Became the Most Influential Man in the World*, 2018, 215–251.

133 John Paul II, Apostolic Exhortation *Familiaris Consortio*, 22 November 1981, 30.

134 John Paul II, Encyclical *Solitudo Rei Socialis*, 30 December 1987, 25.

135 Tad Szulc, *Pope John Paul II. The Biography*, 1995, 21.

136 John Paul II, Letter *Gratissimam Sane*, 2 February 1994, 21.

137 Carl Bernstein and Marco Politi, *His Holiness. John Paul II and the Hidden History of Our Time*, 1996, 518–524.

138 John Paul II, Letter to the Secretary General of the International Conference on Population and Development, 18 March 1994.

139 *National Catholic Reporter*, 9 September 1994.

140 Hehir in Reich, *Encyclopedia of Ethics*, 1255–1256.

141 For an extended treatment of LS see my 'Pope Francis puts environment above short-term politics', 30 June 2016. at www.paulcollinscatholicwriter.com.au

142 *New York Times*, 20 June 2015.

143 Karl Rahner, *Nature and Grace*, 1963, 10. Jurgen Moltmann, *God in Creation*, 1985.

Chapter 11

144 Quoted in Joseph Emmi, 'The solution for technology problems is

more technology, *The Bridge*, 19 April 2017.

145 Mitchell, Andrew J. and Peter Trawny (eds.), *Heidegger's Black Notebooks: Responses to Anti-Semitism*, 2017.

146 Martin Heidegger, *The Question Concerning Technology and Other Essays*, Engl. trans., 1977.

147 Martin Heidegger, 'Nur noch ein Gott kann uns retten', *Der Spiegel* 30 May 1976. Trans. William J. Richardson in Thomas Sheehan, *Heidegger: The Man and the Thinker*, 1981, 45–67.

148 Thomas Sheehan, *Making Sense of Heidegger: A Paradigm Shift*, 2015.

149 William F. Lynch, *Christ and Prometheus: A New Image of the Secular*, 1970, 23.

150 Quoted in Elizabeth Tooker (Ed), *Native North American Spirituality of the Eastern Woodlands*, 1979, 27.

151 Richard J. Woods, *The Spirituality of the Celtic Saints*, 2000, 182–183.

Bibliography

American Jewish Committee, 'Prospecting the Jewish Future: Population Projections, 2000–2080', *American Jewish Year Book,* 2000.

Attenborough, David, 'Humans are a plague on the earth', *Radio Times,* 22/1/2013.

Australian Academy of Science at www.science.org.au/curious/earth/how-many-people-can-earth-actually-support

Bandarage, Asoka, 'Control cash not people', *Ecologist*, 38/8, October 2008.

Barry, John M., *The Great Influenza. The Story of the Deadliest Pandemic in History*, London, Penguin, 2005.

Barth, Karl, *Church Dogmatics*, Edinburgh, T&T Clark, English trans., 1961, III, 4.

Becker, Ernest, *The Denial of Death*, New York, The Free Press, 1973.

Bernstein, Carl and Politi, Marco, *His Holiness. John Paul II and the Hidden History of Our Time*, New York, Doubleday, 1996.

Berry, Thomas, *The Dream of the Earth*, San Francisco, Sierra Club Books, 1988.

— — 'Contemporary spirituality: the journey of the human community', *Cross Currents*, Summer/Fall 1974, 174–75.

Bricker, Daniel and John Ibbitson, *Empty Planet. The Shock of Global Population Decline*, 2019. Oxford, Signal, 2019.

Brown, Peter, *The World of Late Antiquity*, New York, W.W. Norton, 1989.

Brundage John F. and Shanks, G. Dennis 'Deaths from Bacterial Pneumonia during 1918–19 Influenza Pandemic', *Emerging Infectious Diseases Journal*, Vol 14, no 8, August 2008.

Brundtland, Gro Harlem, Report of World Commission on Environment and Development: Our Common Future at www.un-documents.net/our-common-future.pdf

Calamur, Krishnadev, 'The Region Were ISIS, al-Qaeda and Boko Haram Converge', *The Atlantic*, 5 October 2017.

Chryssavgis, John, 'The Green Patriarch', at www.patriarchate.org/the-green-patriarch

Clarkson, Chris et al., 'Human occupation of northern Australia by 65,000 years ago', *Nature*, 19 July 2017. See also *The Conversation*, 20 July 2017.

Cohen, Joel E., *How Many People Can the Earth Support?* New York, W.W. Norton, 1995.

Collins, Paul, *Absolute Power. How the Pope Became the Most Influential Man in the World*, New York, Public Affairs, 2018.

— —*Believers. Does Australian Catholicism Have a Future?* Sydney, UNSW Press, 2008.

— —*Burn. The epic story of bushfire in Australia,* Crow's Nest, Allen & Unwin, 2003.

— —*Between the Rock and a Hard Place. Being Catholic Today*, Sydney, ABC Books, 2004.

— —*God's Earth. Religion as if matter really mattered*, North Blackburn, Vic., HarperCollins, 1995.

— —*Judgment Day. The struggle for life on earth*, Sydney, University of NSW Press and Maryknoll, NY, Orbis Books, 2010.

— —*The Birth of the West. Rome, Germany, France and the Creation of Europe in the Tenth Century*, New York, Public Affairs, 2013.

Columban Mission Society, *Unjust Genes – Life and Death for Sale*, a DVD and booklet on genetically engineered food. At www.columban.org.au

Connell, K.H., *The Population of Ireland, 1750–1845*, Oxford, Clarendon Press, 1950.

Connelly, Matthew, *Fatal Misconception. The struggle to control world population*, Cambridge, Mass., Harvard University Press, 2008.

Daily, G.C., and Ehrlich, Anne and Paul, 'Optimum Population Size', *Population and Environment*, 15(1994), 469–475.

Dalin, Carole, et al., 'Groundwater depletion embedded in international food trade', *Nature*, 543(2017), 700–704.

Dickman, Chris, 'More than one billion animals killed in Australian bushfires', *News and Opinion*, University of Sydney, 8 January 2020.

Douthat, Ross, *The Decadent Society, How We Became the Victims of Our Own Success,* Avid Reader Press, New York, 2020.

——'Pope Francis' Call to Action Goes Beyond the Environment', *New York Times*, 20 June 2015.

Ehrlich, Paul, *The Population Bomb*, New York, Ballantine Books, 1968.

——and Anne Ehrlich, *The Population Explosion*, New York, Simon and Schuster, 1990.

Emerson, David, 'Biogenic Iron Dust. A novel approach to ocean iron fertilization as a means of large-scale removal of carbon dioxide from the atmosphere', *Frontiers in Marine Science*, 7 February 2019 at www.frontiersin.org/articles/10.3389/fmars.2019.00022/full

Emmi, Joseph, 'The solution for technology problems is more technology, *The Bridge*, 19 April 2017.

Filipovic, Jill, 'Why have four children when you could have seven. Family planning in Niger', *Guardian*, 16 March 2017.

Flannery, Tim, *The Future Eaters. An ecological history of the Australasian lands and people*, Sydney, Reed, 1994.

Freud, Sigmund, *Group Psychology and the Analysis of the Ego*, New York, Bantam Books, 1965.

Glikson, Andrew, 'The methane time bomb', *Energy Procedia*, 146(2018), 23–29.

Goldie, Jenny and Betts, Katherine (Eds), *Sustainable Futures*, Canberra: CSIRO Publishing, 2014.

Golson, Jack et al, *Ten Thousand Years of Cultivation at Kuk Swamp in the Highlands of Papua-New Guinea* at https://press.anu.edu/publications/series/terra-australia/ten-thousand-years-cultivation-kuk-swamp-highlands-papua-new

Gore, Al, *Earth in the Balance: Forging a New Common Purpose*, London, Earthscan, 1992.

Heidegger, Martin, 'Nur noch ein Gott kann uns retten', *Der Spiegel*, 30 May 1976.

——*The Question Concerning Technology and Other Essays*, New York,

Garland Publishing, Engl. trans., 1977.

Herlihy, David, *The Black Death and the Transformation of the West*, Cambridge, Mass., Harvard University Press, 1997.

Hill, Tony 'Can the World Really Set Aside Half of the Planet for Wildlife?' *Smithsonian*, September 2014.

Holmes, Edward, 'COVID-19: Time is now to prepare for the next coronavirus outbreak', 9 April 2020. *University of Sydney, News and Opinion*, at www.sydney.edu.au/news-opinion/news/2020/04/09

International Union for Conservation of Nature, Red List, 'Species Extinction – The Facts' at www.iucn.org/resources/conservation-tools/icun-red-list-threatened-species

Jones, Cheryl, 'Frank Fenner sees no hope for humans', *The Australian*, 16 June 2010.

Journeyman Pictures, 'The Tropical Paradise Being Swallowed by the Pacific' at https://www.journeyman.tv/film/7382

King, Gilbert, 'Where the Buffalo No Longer Roamed', *Smithsonian*, 17 July 2012 at www.smithsonianmag.com/history/where-the-buffalo-no-longer-roamed-3067904/

Kump, Lee and Mann, Michael, *Dire Predictions. A Visual Guide to the Finding of the IPCC*, London, DK Publications, 2015.

Leakey, Richard E. and Lewin, Roger, *People of the Lake. Mankind and Its Beginnings*, New York, Anchor Press/Doubleday, 1978.

Levine, Haggai, et al., 'Temporal trends in sperm count: a systematic review and mega-regression analysis', *Human Reproduction Update*, 23(2017), 646–659 at www.ncbi.nih.gov/pubmed/28981654

Lipka, Michael and Hackett, Conrad, 'Why Muslims are the world's fastest-growing religious group', Pew Research Center, 6 April 2017 at www.pewresearch.org/fact-tank/2017/04/06/why-muslims-are-the-worlds-fastest-growing-religious-group

Lovegrove, Roger, *Silent Fields: The long decline of a nation's wildlife*, Oxford, Oxford University Press, 2007.

Lovelock, James, *Gaia: A New Look at Life on Earth*, Oxford, Oxford University Press, 1979.

——*The Revenge of Gaia: Why the Earth is Fighting Back – and how we can still save humanity?* London, Allen Lane/Penguin, 2007.

Lynch, William F., *Christ and Prometheus: A New Image of the Secular*, Notre Dame, Indiana, University of Notre Dame Press, 1970.

Malthus, Thomas, *An Essay on the Principle of Population*, London, J.M. Dent. 1803 edition.

Man, John, *Atlas of the Year 1000*, London, Penguin Books, 1999.

Martin, Paul, *Twilight of the Mammoths: ice age extinctions and rewilding America*, Berkeley, University of California Press, 2005.

McDonagh, Sean, 'Genetic Engineering is not the Answer', *America*, 2 May 2005.

McEvedy, Colin and Jones, Richard *Atlas of World Population History*, Harmondsworth, Penguin Books, 1978.

McKie, Robin, 'Scientists trace 2002 Sars virus to colony of cave-dwelling bats in China', *The Guardian*, 10 December 2017.

McMichael, A.J., *Planetary Overload. Global Environmental Change and the Health of the Human Species*, Cambridge, Cambridge University Press, 1993.

McNeill, William H., *Population and Politics since 1750*, Charlottesville, University Press of Virginia, 1990.

Mitchell, Andrew J., and Peter Trawny (eds.), *Heidegger's Black Notebooks: Responses to Anti-Semitism*, New York, Columbia University Press, 2017.

Moltmann, Jurgen, *God in Creation*, Engl. Trans., London, SCM, 1986.

Monbiot, George, 'Only rebellion will prevent an ecological apocalypse', *The Guardian*, 15 April 2019.

— —'Neoliberalism – the ideology at the root of all our problems', *The Guardian*, 15 April 2016.

National Wildlife Foundation, *Reversing America's Wildlife Crisis*, 29 March 2018 at www.nwf.org/ReversingWildlifeCrisis

Noonan, John T., *Contraception. A History of Its Treatment by the Catholic Theologians and Canonists*, Cambridge, Mass., Harvard University Press, 1968.

Norgaard, Kari, *Living in Denial: Climate Change, Emotions and Everyday Life*, Cambridge, Mass., MIT Press, 2011.

Optimum Population Trust, 'Modest Footprint Carrying Capacity as calculated from Ecological Footprints of Nations Data; Calculations of Human Population Sustainability by countries' at www. optimumpopulation.org

Owen, David, *Thylacine. The Tragic Tale of the Tasmanian Tiger*, Crow's Nest, NSW, Allen & Unwin, 2003.

Paddle, Robert, *The Last Tasmania Tiger. The history and Extinction of the Thylacine*, Cambridge, Cambridge University Press, 2000.

Patrinacos, Nicon D., *The Orthodox Church on Birth Control*, Garwood, NJ, Graphic Arts Press, 1975.

Pison, Gilles, 'Is the Earth over-populated?' The Conversation (Australia) 31 October 2017.

Pope Francis, Encyclical Letter, *Laudato si' On care for our common home*, English trans., Strathfield, NSW, St. Paul's Publications, 2015.

Qing Ke et al., 'China's shift from population control to population quality. Implications for Neurology' at www.ncbi.nlm.nib.gov/pmc/articles/PMC4999320/

Rahner, Karl, *Nature and Grace*, London, Sheed & Ward, 1963.

Rand Corporation (2002), 'International Family Planning Programs: Criticisms and Responses' at www.rand.org/pubs/research_briefs/RB5063/index1.html

Reich, Warren T., (Ed), *The Encyclopedia of Bioethics*, New York, Macmillan, 1978, Vol 3.

Rieff, Philip, *The Triumph of the Therapeutic. The Uses of Faith after Freud*, Chicago: University of Chicago Press, 1966.

Roosevelt, Theodore, *African Game Trails; An Account of the African Wanderings of an American Hunter-Naturalist*, London, John Murray, 1909.

Roser, Max, 'Twice as Long—life expectancy round the world', *Our World in Data*, 8 October 2018.

Rynne, Xavier, *The Third Session. The debates and decrees of Vatican Council II September 14 to November 21, 1964*, London, Faber and Faber, 1965.

Schwartz, Richard H., *Judaism and Global Survival*, New York, Lantern Books, 2002.

Scott, Susan and Duncan, Christopher, *Return of the Black Death*, Chichester, Wiley, 2003.

Sengupta, Pallav et al., 'Evidence in decreasing sperm count in African population from 1965 to 2015', *African Health Sciences*, 17(2017).

Sheehan, Thomas, *Heidegger: The Man and the Thinker*, Chicago, Precedent Publishing, 1981.

――*Making Sense of Heidegger: A Paradigm Shift*, London, Rowman and Littlefield, 2015.

Somerville, Keith, 'Why it's not all about security as West beefs up military in Africa's Sahel', *The Conversation* (UK), 27 October 2016.

――'Explainer: the role of foreign military forces in Niger', *The Conversation* (UK), 9 September 2018.

Steffen, Will et al., 'The Anthropocene: are humans now overwhelming the great forces of nature?' *Ambio* (Royal Swedish Academy of Sciences) 36(2008), 616.

Steiner, George, *Heidegger*, London, HarperCollins, second ed., 1992.

Szulc, Tad, *Pope John Paul II. The Biography*, New York, Scribner, 1995.

Teilhard de Chardin, Pierre, *The Phenomenon of Man*, New York, Harper and Row, 1959.

Tooker, Elizabeth (Ed), *Native North American Spirituality of the Eastern Woodlands*, New York, Paulist Press. 1979.

van der Kaars, Sander et al., 'Humans rather than climate the primary cause of Pleistocene megafaunal extinction in Australia', *Nature Communications*, 20 January 2017.

Vidal, John 'Cut world population and redistribute resources, expert urges', *The Guardian*, 26 April 2012.

――'World needs to stabilise population and cut consumption, says Royal Society', *The Guardian*, 26 April 2012.

Wang Fang, 'The End of China's One-Child Policy', *Studies in Family Planning*, 30 March 2016.

White, Lynn, 'The Historical Roots of the Ecological Crisis', *Science*, 155(1967), 1203–1207.

Wilson, Edward O., 'The Global Solution to Extinction', *The New York Times*, 12 March 2016.

— —*The Future of Life*, New York, Alfred A. Knopf, 2002.

— —*Half-Earth: Our Planet's Fight for Life*, New York, W.W. Norton, 2016.

Woinarski, John, et al., 'A hidden toll: Australia's cats kill about 650 million reptiles a year', *The Conversation*, 26 June 2018.

Woods, Richard J., *The Spirituality of the Celtic Saints*, Maryknoll, NY, Orbis Books, 2000.

World Population Review at www.worldpopulationreview.com/countries/total-fertility-rate

Worrall, Simon, 'When did the First Americans Arrive? It's complicated', *National Geographic*, 9 June 2018.

Yeoman, Barry, 'Why the Passenger Pigeon Went Extinct', *Audubon Magazine*, May–June 2014 at www.audubon.org/magazine/may-june-2014/why-passenger-pigeon-went-extinct

Zimmerman, Judith and Trainin, Barbara (Eds), *Jewish Population: Renascence or Oblivion*, New York, Federation of Jewish Philanthropies of New York, 1979.

Index

www.ingramcontent.com/pod-product-compliance
Ingram Content Group Australia Pty Ltd
76 Discovery Rd, Dandenong South VIC 3175, AU
AUHW020841060325
407965AU00004B/31

9 781922 669216